LUNGEING THE HORSE AND RIDER

LUNGEING THE HORSE AND RIDER

SHEILA INDERWICK
Illustrations by 'Tiptaft'

DAVID & CHARLES
Newton Abbot   London   North Pomfret (Vt)

British Library Cataloguing in Publication Data
Inderwick, Sheila
Lungeing the horse and rider.
1. Horse-training
I. Title
636.1'08'8   SF287
ISBN 0–7153–7370–6

First published 1977
Second impression 1978
Third impression 1980
Fourth impression 1981
Fifth impression 1982
Sixth impression 1983

Printed in Great Britain
by Redwood Burn Limited
for David & Charles (Publishers) Limited
Brunel House Newton Abbot Devon

Published in the United States of America
by David & Charles Inc
North Pomfret Vermont 05053 USA

CONTENTS

PART ONE

LUNGEING THE HORSE

1 BEGINNINGS AND AIMS

Anyone who writes a book dealing with the training of horses must do so in the knowledge that the past has been poorly documented and very little real research has yet been undertaken. It is a subject tied to tradition and legend rather than the written word. Certainly, few writers on equestrian matters have paid much attention to lungeing and there is little to guide those who wish to school their own horses. The methods used vary considerably and are often the product of practice and experimentation rather than literary study. From the earliest days, man must have discovered that the only way to hold, much less stop, an impetuous young horse, was for the man leading him to pull him round in a circle, and thus lungeing was born. The derivation of the word is undoubtedly from the French, *longe* – a halter – and *longer* – to run alongside, and lungeing in English is still sometimes spelled with an 'o' instead of a 'u'.

Centuries later, there are still few who really appreciate how vital early lessons on the lunge can be to the whole future of their horse. Until the last war, breaking and backing was almost invariably left to stud grooms or itinerant bands of colt breakers who travelled the countryside each spring handling young horses. As soon as they had got the buck out of them by chasing them round on a rope, younger members of the family were thrown up. Some of these breakers were wonderful natural horsemen, but time was money and it was often a case of breaking their mount's spirit sufficiently for the more elderly stud groom to take over, rather than any pretence at training. Once this stage was reached, the stud groom would start by putting on a dumb jockey and a key mouthing bit and drive the youngster on two reins attached to the snaffle. He then drove him either in a circle, which is known as long-reining, or round the summer lanes before the hunters came up. This encouraged the colt to go forward, face everyday hazards, and even jump small ditches, etc, before he was asked to carry weight. This method had much to commend it and was, of course, essential if the animal was destined for harness work. Therefore, very little lungeing, as we know it today, was ever included in early training. Those who did practise it, as well as long-reining, were often illiterate and worked mostly from hearsay or legend. The only standardised methods were to be found in cavalry regiments, famous schools such as the Spanish Riding School, and in the circus. It is directly due to their teaching that methods which, in the past, had been rough and ready means to an end, became an art to be studied and used throughout a horse's life.

Nowadays, far more lungeing than long-reining is practised although the latter may well return now that driving is becoming so popular again. It is not the point of this book to discuss long-reining except to say that it requires great expertise if forward impulsion and natural posture are not to be lost.

Lungeing, however, is within the power of anyone seriously committed to training horses. It has five main purposes:

1 The training of young horses.
2 The re-training of spoilt horses.
3 The exercising of horses which cannot be ridden.
4 The training of riders.
5 Advanced work in hand.

2 ESSENTIAL EQUIPMENT

Tack

All tack used when working a horse on the lunge should be light but well made, well cared for and very strong, as it is often subject to sudden strain. If it is not supple and well fitting it quickly causes sores, especially on young horses, with consequential pain, loss of attention and, finally, disobedience.

The following are required: either a strong lungeing roller with at least two rings securely fastened to each side or saddle with a well oiled, folded-leather girth or nylon-string girth. This should be able to withstand the pressure exerted when a horse bucks, but should not be too long or it may interfere with the attachment of the side-reins. These are usually of leather, about 1½in wide and 5ft long. One end has a buckle and a strap with at least 15 holes for adjustment; the other end requires a round-ended spring clip. The spring should face outwards when fixed to the bit to prevent any chafing of the horse's lips. Most saddlers make them the other way round and it is advisable to have this changed. The use and fitting of side-reins will be dealt with later, in Chapter 4.

The usual bridle is a simple snaffle one with a fairly thick, single-jointed, smooth snaffle, preferably with cheek pieces and keepers, and a drop noseband. This should be fitted as for an ordinary cavesson noseband, ie approximately four fingers width above the upper edge of the nostril so as not to inhibit the respiratory passage in any way. The back strap is then fastened below the bit. If you intend to ride the horse immediately after lungeing, the reins may be left on but it is advisable to remove them if working unbroken or very boisterous horses, as they can come loose and cause an accident.

If reins are retained, they should never be placed under the stirrups or fixed to the saddle in any way. They should either be twisted twice round the horse's neck or, having been placed over the neck, one rein should be twisted around the other under the neck and the throat strap put through the resulting loop (Figure 1). This has the advantage of not allowing the reins to interfere in any way with the bit.

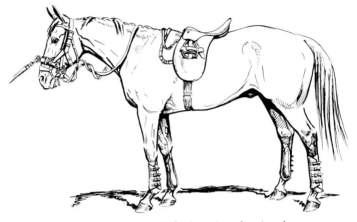

Figure 1   A young horse equipped for lungeing, showing the correct way of twisting the reins to keep them out of the way

The cavesson is placed over the bridle, making sure that it fits the horse and that no mane is caught between it and the top of the bridle. Correctly made cavessons are no longer very heavy but take the form of a padded drop noseband with a metal fitting, jointed at both sides, fitted on the front of the noseband. Three swivel rings are attached to this band and the lunge rein is invariably fixed to the centre ring. The cavesson has a cheek strap which should always be tight enough to prevent the cavesson pulling round and touching the horse's outside eye. Cavessons are usually fitted above the bit if the horse is already wearing a drop noseband, in which case there is less interference with the bit if the back strap of the cavesson goes under the cheek piece of the bridle, though this is a matter of opinion. However, when lungeing a very strong colt, it may be necessary to fit the lungeing cavesson as a drop noseband in order to give a greater degree of control. At all times the noseband must be tightly fitted to prevent rubbing.

Boots should always be used all round as, even with unshod horses, knocks can occur. They also act as support to the tendons which are under considerable strain when working on a circle. Polo boots, which cover the fetlock joints, are probably the best protection but any boots are preferable to bandages which can cause serious accidents should they come undone, or become too tight if they get wet when in use.

The lunge rein should be about 30ft long and made of either linen or nylon webbing about 1½–2in wide. Some people use lamp wick which is both soft and light and equally strong but tends to curl and does not always slip freely. It is very dangerous to use rope which can cause serious burns if pulled through the hands. There should be a large loop at one end of the rein and either a buckle or a spring clip attached by a swivel joint at the other. It is most important that this swivel is light but strong and free-moving because otherwise the rein will twist in use.

Finally a lunge whip is needed. The type of whip is very much a case of personal preference, but it should have a light and well balanced stock, preferably a thin plaited thong about 8ft long with a lash on the end. This is attached to the stock by a loop of raw hide. Heavy whips with a swivel joint at the top of the stock are really carters' whips and not suitable for serious lungeing.

Use of the Whip

From the start, the whip should be thought of as an aid to training and not a means of punishment and it is not necessary to have one of sufficient length to reach the horse at all times. It is however, an art in itself to use a whip correctly – an art which should certainly be well practised before you attempt to train horses on the lunge. It is essential to have a well balanced whip which can be held lightly in a relaxed hand without fixing the fingers in a strong grip, otherwise the tension created will be at the expense of dexterity. Nor should the point be held up, as when driving in a vehicle, but pointed downwards with the thong resting on the ground. The thong should then be used to follow the horse quietly round the circle, each movement coming mostly from the wrist with a slight contra-action just before the completion of each lift. This creates a slight ripple in the thong, resulting in a small crack of the lash and also ensuring that the thong does not get twisted or knotted in any way. It is, of course, essential that you should be able to use a whip equally well in either hand.

A horse must never be frightened of the whip but must respect it and once or twice it may be necessary to let him feel it. In this case it should be used just above the inside hock, again with a small flicking movement and with only the lash making contact. It takes a lot of practice to be sure of doing this accurately and it is a good idea to experiment on inanimate things such as thistle heads, gate posts, fallen leaves, etc, until you can be sure of dropping the lash of your whip exactly where you wish it to go. You will find that, by concentrating the eyes and thoughts solely on the spot you wish to reach, it gradually becomes easier to attain. It cannot be stressed too highly that expertise in the use of the whip should be mastered before lungeing any horse.

When not in use, the whip should be brought quietly round to the back of the trainer and held under the arm with the thong trailing, so keeping it away from the feet of both trainer and his horse (Figure 2).

Figure 2 When not in use the whip should be brought gently round the trainer's back and held under the arm

For the same reason, and also because a good whip becomes a treasured possession and is easily broken, the whip should never be placed on the floor while handling the horse. Nor should a whip ever be raised or used in anger, as it only creates confusion and fear in the horse's mind and it is all too easy to flick an eye, with the risk of subsequent blindness, or to get the thong caught under the horse's dock and in the ensuing chaos have both horse and man injured. It is wiser never to lift the point of the whip beyond shoulder level, except as a signal to the horse either to halt or not to come inwards on the circle, in which case it should be held upright and very still.

Should it be necessary to hit a horse with a whip, the overall length of which is less than the length of the lunge rein in use, it is better to take a quiet step towards the horse to reach him rather than to reduce the circle which might well add to the difficulties and/or disobedience of the animal. The very fact that you move towards the horse may well provide sufficient stimulus to make using the whip unnecessary.

After use all whips should be wiped down with saddle soap and hung from the top on a whip-reel with the thong loosely tied to the stock.

3 TRAINER'S TECHNIQUE

Working a horse on the lunge requires all the attributes and the same knowledge and skill as is demanded when mounted. In fact, put rather more fancifully, you 'ride from the ground' with the added advantage of being able to watch the effect of training as it progresses. Self-discipline, patience and, above all, concentration are of the utmost importance at all times. It is essential to establish a mental 'rapport' with the horse not only to counteract the lack of the physical contact, which is present when riding, but also to keep him attentive and listening for your commands. This happy state can never be achieved unless the trainer is able to eliminate all outside distractions and thoughts from his mind and devote all his willpower and concentration to his horse. After the first introduction to working on the lunge, it is always best to work alone in some secluded place and, above all, never to carry on a conversation with, or worse still, teach another person while lungeing.

Arena

The choice of surface for a lunge ring is very important as slippery, unlevel going does not help concentration. It is also surprisingly easy for a young horse to fall while working on a circle, even in an indoor school, if the going is too deep or heavy.

Nowadays, the most suitable surface for the floor of an indoor school is usually considered to be 75 per cent wood shavings and 25 per cent sand with sufficient agricultural salt just to keep it damp without constant watering. Lungeing on an over-dry surface soon creates clouds of dust which are not only harmful to horse and trainer but are a distraction and may discourage the horse from lowering his head. It is, however, a mistake always to lunge in a school or in the same place, for that way lies boredom and the subsequent disobedience which is so often its product. Once the horse is under control, any well drained corner of a field is suitable. If the need for some demarcation is felt necessary an excellent enclosure can be erected by using sheep hurdles leaning against each other in pairs (Figure 3). These have

Figure 3 A good makeshift enclosure made from sheep hurdles

the advantage of being portable and easily erected and, because they slope away from the horse, are unlikely to be touched by him. Where possible this outdoor manège should be rectangular, not round, so that the horse can be worked on straight lines and over jumps, etc.

Stance

While lungeing, it is important that the trainer adopts a posture and stance equivalent to his position in the saddle. It may sound pedantic but good posture leads to relaxation and calmness, from which come strength and quick thinking. The trainer should stand in the centre of the circle with his waist up, his shoulders flat, his head high and his eyes level (Figure 4). The upper arms should hang lightly downwards towards the hips and the hands, whether holding the rein or the whip, should be soft and flexible and roughly at right angles to the body. The legs should be slightly apart and the knees relaxed. In this position,

Figure 4   Correct stance for the trainer

with the weight equally distributed, any sudden pull by the horse can be absorbed by bending the knees and controlling the weight of the body. If, however, the would-be trainer stands off-balance with hunched shoulders and stiff limbs, as is all too often the case, he will easily be pulled forward and lose control (Figure 5).

Figure 5   (a) The over-attentive, unbalanced trainer . . .

(b) and what can easily result

Use of the Lunge Rein

The lunge rein should be fastened by the buckle or the spring clip to the centre ring on the cavesson because its main purpose is to control forward movement, not the bend of the horse's neck. The other two rings are intended for very advanced work in hand and in the pillars although, in former times, a rein was frequently attached to be used by riders in conjunction with the bit and in place of the bridoon (Figure 6). The rein should come in a straight line to the trainer's hand

Figure 6   Sketch from an illustration in the Duke of Newcastle's book on *Horsemanship*, 1743

and he should adjust its length by taking it up in loops. It is essential that this is done from the trainer's end towards the horse, not the other way round. Unless the loop nearest the horse lies on top of the others, it can not easily be slipped and this could result in the rein twisting around the trainer's hand or finger with very painful, if not serious, results – it has been known for the top of a finger to be pulled off in such circumstances. For this reason, never lunge without fairly loose-fitting gloves; never wear spurs which could become entangled in either the rein or the whip; and never place rein or whip on the floor except in extreme circumstances which will be dealt with later. The rein should not be allowed to become slack when not in use but be taken up in neat loops as the trainer moves towards the horse's head.

Position

The trainer should stand at an angle of roughly 45–50° to the horse's forehand and concentrate on the movement of the horse's quarters rather than the head and neck, ie with his back slightly towards the direction in which the horse is travelling. In other words, the horse's head should be just in front of the trainer's leading shoulder (Figure 7).

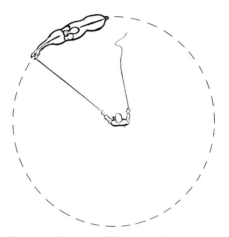

Figure 7   Showing the angle of the trainer in relation to the horse

In this way, the trainer can be sure that the horse is going forward freely and not just setting his pace to that of his instructor. It also gives greater control should any evasions, such as stopping, running backwards, etc, occur. In fact, should a trainer allow the horse to get behind the 'aids', ie the whip or the rein, the animal nearly always loses his impulsion, if not actually stops. For some reason, horses dislike facing

20

up to human eyes, as is often obvious when leading or when loading them into horseboxes (Figure 8).

Except when lungeing a very green horse, when it is sometimes necessary to describe a small circle, the trainer should try to remain

Figure 8   Eye contact with a human handler makes horses nervous

stationary in the centre of the circle and to rotate on one heel by stepping forward and slightly across with the other leg. It is generally accepted that the rotating leg is the one nearest to the direction in which the horse is moving. The whole movement should be carried out in co-ordination with the whip and should be quiet and unhurried. The lunge rein, correctly looped, is held in the hand nearest the horse's

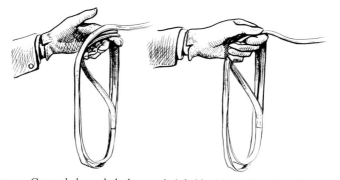

Figure 9   Correctly looped, the lunge rein is held with the thumb on the topmost loop

21

head, with the thumb on the topmost loop so it can be slipped if necessary (Figure 9).

In this way the trainer, the horse, the whip and the rein form a triangle and, while this is maintained, the horse might be said to be 'on the aids' as in riding, except of course that the whip replaces the leg, and the lunge rein, the controlling hand.

It cannot be stressed too often that everything which is taught on the lunge should directly relate to what will happen once the horse is mounted.

Use of Voice

One of the most important aids is the use of the voice. What matters is the tone rather than the actual words but these must be distinct, never vary except in tone, and be as few as possible. Horses have very acute hearing and there is never any need to raise the voice for normal commands – in fact a horse is more apt to attend if he has to listen for a quietly spoken 'walk on' rather than a shouted order which may well cause him to throw up his head and jump forward. If you start with quiet but distinct commands, you still have a chance to make them stronger should the need arise. No-one but the inexpert or the exhibitionist shouts at a horse when riding so it should not be done when lungeing.

Introducing the Horse to Lunge Work

Assuming that a young horse has been well handled, lead from both sides and accustomed to both saddle and bridle, it is comparatively easy to commence lunge work. Many trainers do this without assistance but it is probably wiser, especially with highly strung horses, to have a well trained helper on the first occasion.

The horse should wear a snaffle bridle with a dropped noseband and a well fitting lungeing cavesson. If the reins are left on the bridle they should be twisted and held by the throat lash, as described earlier. Either a lunge roller with side rings or a saddle may be used. If a numnah is needed it should be attached to the saddle or roller as, without the rider's weight to anchor it, it easily works backwards. The stirrups can be removed but, if the horse is to be mounted later, it is acceptable to run them up. To prevent the irons from rubbing the saddle or slipping down, they should be run up on the outside instead of the inside, of the leathers, the ends of which are then threaded through the irons, under the top of the leather and out over the side of the stirrup irons. The free ends of the stirrup leathers are threaded through the resulting loops (Figure 10). The side-reins are then attached

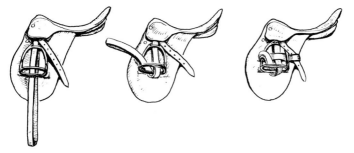

Figure 10   The accepted method of running up stirrups when lungeing

by threading the strap ends under the girth straps, then back over the first and under the second strap – once the girth is tight they seldom slip (Figure 11). Alternatively, they can be threaded through the ring on the roller. In either case, they should be a little above half way up the horse's sides, ie more or less in a straight line from the mouth to the girth when the horse is standing naturally. Initially, they should be fastened into the longest hole and both should always be of equal

Figure 11   Correct fitting of side-reins through girth straps

23

length and height. This is best checked by standing in front of the horse and pulling both reins forwards for comparison. They should never be attached to the bit until the horse is actually working on the lunge but should be crossed over the withers and clipped, either to the D's on the saddle or roller, or to the stirrup irons. Simply clipping them together over the horse's neck is not advised as there is the danger that they might slip down to one side and a playful youngster could get a foreleg through the loop. As stressed earlier, protective boots covering the fetlock joints should always be worn.

Once the horse is correctly tacked up, the lunge rein is fitted to the centre ring of the cavesson and the horse led on this to the school. The principle of always leading from the cavesson and not the bit is well worth continuing throughout the horse's life. Not only does it protect his mouth but also instils from the start the recognition that contact with the bit is an aid to which he must attend, not a casual or an accidental annoyance. It is well worth the extra trouble of slipping a cavesson over the bridle, even when leading a well trained, older horse, to ensure that his intelligent 'listening' in response to the contact of the bit is never dissipated or goes unrewarded by the expected direction or demand.

Use of Assistant

In the past, most instructors advocated that any helper should lead the horse from the outside of the circle with the trainer standing in the middle and driving the horse forward with the whip. Not only is this very hard work for the helper but it immediately sets up confusion in the horse's mind for, until then, he has been used to being lead from one side only and on a fairly short rein. For this reason, it is now more often the practice to let the helper lead the horse, in the usual way, from the inside of the circle but with the lunge rein passing through his hand to the trainer in the middle. At the same time, he may carry a short whip or stick in the hand nearest the horse to gently encourage him to move forward and slightly in front of him (Figure 12). There being nothing unusual about this, the horse soon settles and the helper then starts to move inwards towards the trainer in the middle by gradually decreasing the track of his circle and allowing the lunge rein to lengthen. At the same time, he encourages the horse to remain on the larger circle by pointing his whip at him and keeping him walking quietly forward. As soon as he is within reasonable distance of the middle, he can let go of the rein and slip behind the trainer, who then takes over. Once behind the trainer, the helper continues to turn with him and is out of harm's way as far as the whip is concerned. If and when all is peaceful, the helper's work is done and it is quite easy for him to leave by waiting until the horse has passed him and then walking out of the circle. During this introduction there should be no conversation between trainer and helper and all commands should be given by the trainer to the horse, as it is his voice to which the animal must become accustomed and learn to obey.

Figure 12   Lungeing with an assistant

It is unlikely that a helper will be needed again if the first introduction to lunge work is carried out quietly and expertly. It is worth considering briefing the helper beforehand with the aid of an older horse, as a mistake at this stage can sometimes hinder all future training programmes.

All this initial work should be carried out without the use of side-reins and these should not even be considered until the horse can be worked in trot. This point will be discussed again in Chapter 4 but, even with more advanced horses, many trainers allow a few minutes freedom on the lunge to warm up and get rid of any excessive exuberance before attaching side-reins.

Certainly with young horses it is best always to start and sometimes finish on the easiest rein which is nearly always the left. However, if it is a case of really too much misplaced enthusiasm on the horse's part, this can sometimes be inhibited, if not completely stopped, by changing onto the more difficult rein. Provided that the trainer is still in control, such high spirits at the beginning of a lesson are better encouraged than dominated and may well prevent evasions arising later on.

It should always be remembered that work on the circle, particularly if the horse is young or unfit, is very demanding both of energy and mental powers and should never be continued for long periods of time. Ten to fifteen minutes on each rein is about the limit for older horses and considerably less in the early stages of training. This, of course, refers to really active work and the time can be longer if periods of rest, without side-reins and at a free walk, are included. However, it is probably wiser to finish after a short period of active but steady work than to continue at a slow pace for too long which may allow boredom to take over from concentration.

4 PRINCIPLES OF TRAINING

Once the horse has started to walk and trot quietly round the trainer on a large circle, serious work can commence. Training on the lunge has four basic objects: firstly to make a horse fit and strong enough to be ridden; secondly to make him quiet enough to be safe to ride; thirdly to accustom him to the use of the voice, and eventually the aids; and finally to expand and enhance all his natural abilities, both mental and physical, to their maximum. To achieve these aims the trainer must be familiar with the basic principles of training.

When living naturally, even the present-day domesticated horse spends most of his time either grazing or resting and occasionally sleeping. He moves slowly, mostly at the walk or, when actually grazing, by moving one or at the most two legs at a time, as he changes balance towards the particular piece of pasture he fancies. His first line of defence is flight and even a day-old foal has great powers of acceleration but it is rarely sustained and, apart from fits of playfulness, horses lead a rather sedentary life. Nevertheless, they are wonderful athletes and have great stamina, endurance and, not least, intelligence. These three attributes are latent in all young horses but it requires great care to develop them for the use of man. At all times, training must be based on natural principles and governed by the fitness, mental as well as physical, of the horse. Any trainer who tries to exploit this or who takes short cuts will lay up troubles both for himself and his horse in the future.

Basic Theory

The theory of training is to allow the animal to move forward with natural rhythm and balance and, therefore, posture. This leads to relaxed, supple movements, flexibility and, ultimately, attentiveness.

In this receptive state the whole outline of the horse becomes long: the head carriage is low as when about to graze, the long muscles of the back and neck are relaxed and swinging, and the quarters supple (Figure 13).

Figure 13   The basic outline of all novice horses, with a long, low posture

This should be the basic outline of all novice horses, both on the lunge and when ridden. The trainer can then gradually ask for more flexibility of the quarters which lengthens the stride and brings the hind legs a little further under the horse's body. This allows more of the weight to be placed on the hind legs, so lightening the forehand and raising the neck and head. This again is the perfectly natural effect of the gathering together of all the horse's muscular power over a smaller base which is somewhat loosely called collection and can frequently be seen when colts are at play.

The trainer's object is slowly to build up his horse's muscular powers and his understanding until he can reproduce all the beauty and grace of his natural movements while being ridden. The acme of all such training is work above the ground, ie the high-school leaps such as a *capriole*, but few men or horses ever attain it. However, with years of consistent, careful training which does not go faster or beyond the dictates of nature, many can achieve the high degree of collection demanded for *piaffe* and *passage*. To reach this standard all work on the lunge must relate completely to work under saddle and takes about five or six years to establish.

Most basic work is done at the trot, partly because it is in two time and equal sided – that is the horse springs from one pair of diagonal legs to the other and so the balance is fairly stable. It also has more natural impulsion than the walk without being too active to control when dealing with a young horse.

The youngster should therefore be asked to go forward into trot by the use of the voice backed up by a slight flick of the whip towards his quarters. At this stage, do not expect instant reactions or true transitions. It is enough if the horse moves forward into trot and continues at that pace until asked to walk. Few young horses are fit enough or sufficiently well balanced to work in canter on a circle, but should the horse offer canter instead of trot, it is often wiser to accept this rather than constantly check the desire to go forward. At the same time it should be remembered that the canter pace is often an easier one for the horse and so is sometimes used to evade the harder work at the trot. One way to stop this without actually checking the horse is to turn to face him and, dropping the point of the whip, just allow him to 'run down' and then start again in trot. Other methods will be dealt with later in Chapter 7.

Once the horse has learned to go quietly forward at the trot the trainer can start worrying about the rhythm. At this stage you may not see a very good length of stride but rhythm is absolutely essential from the start. Rhythm is natural to all living things in one form or another and should be paramount in the thoughts of all trainers. If movements become irregular nothing further should be attempted until the cause has been discovered and, if possible, corrected. In young horses, most loss of rhythm springs from mental tension and/or fear of the whip, and shows itself in hurried, irregular steps. This is a fault of the trainer and can easily be corrected by allowing the animal to relax and by the use of calming words. If irregularity continues, it may be that the horse is not describing a true circle with all four feet in the same track; he may be carrying his quarters to one side or be falling onto one shoulder. These faults should improve with work and as balance becomes established. Persistent unlevelness or loss of rhythm can also result from unsoundness or arthritic conditions of the spine and in these cases veterinary advice should be sought.

Fitting the Side-reins

Once the horse has learned to trot quietly round on a large circle and has been allowed a few minutes to settle down, the side-reins can be attached to the bit and serious work started. Remembering that the overall outline of a novice horse should be long and low, it is essential that the length of the side-reins is dictated by the horse, not the trainer. Ideally, in the early stages, they should be sufficiently long for contact to be made with the bit only when the horse relaxes and lowers his head. This movement is both downward and forward with the nose well in front of the vertical and is the result of suppleness induced by the calmness, impulsion and regularity of the pace. It should not be confused with the result of a lazy or dwelling trot in which the impulsion does not really go forward or through the horse but is dissipated in mental and/or physical tension. In this case, if the horse lowers his head at all, it is usually backwards towards his chest and away from the bit, and is frequently the result of the side-reins being shortened too early.

It should be stressed that in all stages of training, the horse must make contact with the bit not the other way round. In this way the horse gradually realizes that, when he lowers his head, he will always find the bit in the same place. He will not be frightened of it but will learn to accept it and finally to seek it and even gently chew it. It is at this moment that the trainer needs to exercise all his skill and tact. He must be able to co-ordinate the driving force of the voice and whip with the moment that the horse starts to reach forward for the bit. At the same time, he must gently ease the tension on the lunge rein to allow the horse all the freedom it requires with its head and neck, and to encourage it to lower the head. All these actions require split-second timing and are so slight as to be practically unnoticeable but, if the impulsion is not maintained and even slightly increased, as the horse finds the bit, he will soon learn either to withdraw from it or begin to lean on it. As long as the regular, free-going trot is maintained balance will not be so easily lost nor will the horse drop the bit. He will gradually learn to accept it and to adopt the long, low posture which is perfectly natural in a young horse. For some reason, most horses seem to start to lower their heads each time they reach a particular section of the circle. A clever trainer should anticipate this and try gradually to increase the duration of time that the horse's head is lowered until the required posture is maintained throughout each revolution.

If this act of seeping the bit is carefully taught at this early stage, it will remain as an invaluable aid for the rest of the horse's life should tension arise. When offered a long rein or when contact is abandoned, the horse will instinctively lower his head and relax without losing his balance.

The Importance of the Circle

Unfortunately, it is by no means easy to get a horse to describe a true circle on each rein, yet this is the basis of all training. Unless the horse is, as near as possible equally supple and muscularly developed on both sides, it will be impossible for him to make full use of his powers when ridden. Unnatural stress on one or other of his limbs may well develop with eventual breakdown to follow.

The importance of the trainer standing still in the middle of the circle and revolving on one heel becomes clear. Only in this way can he be sure that the horse is tracing a true circle and is working

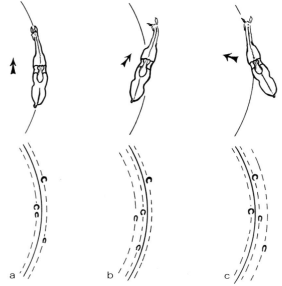

Figure 14   (a) A straight horse with the hind feet following in the track of the fore feet
(b) Pulling out of the circle, incorrect on three tracks
(c) Incorrect on three tracks, falling into the circle

equally well on both reins. Another way of testing this is to check that the imprint of the hind feet follow the same track as those of the fore feet (Figure 14). This is known in dressage terms as a horse being 'straight', ie the impulsion, when produced, can go straight through the horse to the rider's hands. This straightness is essential in the training of a youngster and applies whether he is going on a circle, through a bend or just in a straight line. If the quarters do not follow the track of the forehand, but are carried to one side, a lot of the impulsion is dissipated, usually through the opposite shoulder and balance is lost. Clearly, work on two tracks, such as shoulder-in and half passes, should never be attempted until the horse has truly learned to go forward on one track.

Unfortunately, no creature on this earth seems to be completely equal sided and horses, like men, show a preference either to the left or right. This is usually the former and man tends to exaggerate this by being mostly right handed and therefore leading his horse from the left side. No-one really seems to know why such preference should be but it is a fact which is rarely, if ever, completely eliminated. The most a trainer can do is to make his horse so supple that he is able to use every muscle to its maximum effect.

This preference is immediately noticeable when a horse is first lunged on a circle because, unlike most other animals, the horse's spine has practically no lateral flexion at all. To negotiate the track of a circle, he has to call into play his immensely flexible forehand and his ability to close up the large angles in the framework of his quarters. Thus, by using the long muscles in his croup and hind legs, the horse can bring one hind leg forward and slightly under his body and onto the line of the circle. This causes a displacement of weight forwards and slightly towards the outside shoulder which is moved forward allowing the inside shoulder and foreleg to come onto the line of the circle. Hence there is muscular lateral flexion with the inside or concave side being slightly more contracted than the outer. In this way a horse can describe a circle on one track despite his mainly rigid spine.

This will usually be quite easy for him when turning to his preferred soft or concave side but difficulties appear when the animal is asked to flex his muscles the other way. The problem may not be so marked in an unbroken horse, which is sufficiently supple to disguise it, but in some older horses a change onto the stiff rein may have almost paralysing effects, with the horse throwing up his head, trying to stop and appearing almost lame. This one-sided stiffness has frequently been encouraged and established by riders who are themselves very left or right handed and who prefer not to change the diagonal when trotting. A good trainer should recognise these symptoms and not confuse them with disobedience because it may take a long time to get an older or stiff horse sufficiently supple to revolve equally well on both reins.

Bend of Head and Neck

The muscular bend throughout the horse's length, which the trainer seeks, will be dissipated if it does not include bend in the neck as well. This should not exceed and, indeed, should be an integral part of the slight bend obtainable throughout the length of the body. If the eye is drawn to the bend in the horse's neck, rather than the overall outline, the neck is bent too much. This all too easily happens as, unlike the spine, the vertebrae of the horse's neck are extremely flexible and the neck and head together act as a balancing pole for the whole animal. Therefore, if the trainer allows too much weight to fall on the inside shoulder the horse will try to turn his head and neck away from the circle in order to maintain his equilibrium. Efforts to correct this, by pulling on the lunge rein, will only increase the difficulty by placing even more load on the inside shoulder. Some trainers advocate the shortening of the inside side-rein in such cases (Figure 15), but this contradicts the principle that the horse should always make the contact

Figure 15   Shortening one side-rein leads to all sorts of resistances being set up

with the bit not the other way round. If the trainer uses the reins to position a young horse's head and neck, before he has found and learned to accept the bit, all sorts of resistances may be set up, both in the mouth and in the general suppleness of the horse. A horse's usual evasion when one side-rein is shorter than the other is to try to carry his quarters to the outside of the circle which, again, overloads the inside shoulder and so amplifies the original fault of turning the head and neck to the outside of the bend.

If, on the other hand, the side-reins are of equal length and height and the horse is encouraged to step well forward and slightly under his body with the inside hind leg, a good deal of his weight will be transferred diagonally towards the outside shoulder. In turning away from this outside shoulder to maintain his balance, he will bend his head and neck inwards and in line with the rest of his body on the circle. In so doing, as he relaxes and lowers his head, he will make slightly stronger contact with the outside side-rein, that side of his mouth will become moist and the inside side-rein will become looser (Figure 16). In fact, far from being shortened, it will appear to be longer and the bend will have developed from the natural balance and movement of the horse, not from the use of force or artificial aids.

Figure 16   Both side-reins of equal length encourage the horse to relax, lower his head and the inside side-rein will become looser

With most young horses this even bend is usually easy to achieve but with older or stiff horses it is sometimes advisable to allow them to work with an incorrect posture until their general suppleness improves. To help this, they should not be driven forward too strongly

34

at first and may even be allowed to carry their quarters slightly in on the circle with a very light but steady contact with the lunge rein. This helps to take the weight off the inside shoulder and, if done quietly and calmly, the tensions, both mental and physical, begin to subside and the horse will gradually return to the true line of the circle with a soft bend throughout. No-one can really position a stiff horse, except by unacceptable methods, and it is wiser to wait for time and nature to do it for you.

This seeking and acceptance of the outer side-rein is of immense importance to the horse's mounted training. It is an introduction to the passive outside rein, which riders use both to control the pace and to assist the balance of their horses; at the same time the lighter inside rein encourages the horse to bend into the movement with a soft, receptive mouth.

When a young horse can work with a long, low outline, with a supple bend throughout and a consistent but light contact with the outside rein, he is ready to proceed with his further training.

5 PACES AND TRANSITIONS

Until now, all energies have been concentrated on teaching the horse to go forward in a relaxed manner and to find the bit. This has been done at a trot and governed by his age and physical condition. He will also have been worked at a free walk, without the side-reins. As he becomes fitter, more attention must be paid to the purity of the paces and to the transition from one to the other and to the halt. Firstly, it must be realized that impulsion should never be confused with speed – a horse really going forward in *piaffe* does not gain ground but may well create more impulsion than he would at a gallop. True impulsion is one of the most difficult things to describe and often takes years to recognise but one way of summing it up might be to say that it is the co-ordination of willpower and energy. This is transposed into fluid movement by the suppleness of the muscles, the elasticity of the tendons and the flexibility of the joints. In this way, each step is given its true value. As a foot touches the ground, the appropriate flexion takes place, allowing that limb first to sink downwards into the ground and then to rebound with added energy. Provided that there is no stiffness, the harder the ground is struck, the greater will be the recoil and subsequent elevation, and the longer the leg is in the air, the more time there is to lengthen the stride. This in turn allows the horse to cover a greater distance in the same time and in the same rhythm.

Nowadays, four paces of the trot and canter are recognised and referred to as working, medium, collected and extended but for early work on the lunge only the first need be considered. The name is in itself descriptive and this pace is well within the capabilities of any supple horse. It must be well defined with light, rounded steps and the imprint of the hind foot at least coming up to that left by the fore foot. The length of stride is less than that which should later be demanded for a medium trot but more than that required for collection. It must always appear easy and natural and it is the trainer's task to establish this trot by ensuring that the horse always has sufficient impulsion and suppleness to accept it. One of the greatest aids towards this end are the transitions because, whether going into a slower or faster pace, extra impulsion is required if the balance is to be maintained and the paces remain true and rhythmical.

In the first place, transitions are obtained mainly by the use of the voice backed up by the whip, if necessary, and thought should be given to the actual words used. For instance, if 'whoa' is used to ask for a halt, it may be mistaken for 'walk'. It is wiser to use 'halt', which has a strong abrupt sound, and to add the word 'on', ie 'walk on', 'trot on', when referring to paces. This leaves the words 'whoa' or 'steady' as a warning of changes to come. Care must be taken with intelligent horses that, when using words of praise, such as 'good boy', the horse is not allowed to translate this as a command to stop work. If the whip is moved gently towards him at the same time as the remark is made, this problem should not arise. On the other hand, frequent praise without reward soon becomes meaningless. It is wiser to halt the horse and, while keeping him on the track of the circle, walk up to him and make a fuss of him. If this halt is at all prolonged, or if it is used to change onto the other circle, the side-reins should be unclipped from the bit until work is recommenced. It is also wise to reserve any titbits until the end of the lesson when the reins are finally undone, as sugar, etc sometimes encourages the horse to play with the bit instead of quietly accepting it.

It is important that, whether transitions are made from walk to trot, or the other way round, or to halt, the influence is always forward. Horses must not be allowed to run with indefinite quick steps when going into trot or, worse still, to fall back into an irregular, unbalanced walk. Once more, it is the tact and co-ordination of the trainer which can prevent this by keeping the horse between the aids of the whip and the rein and encouraging a very slight increase of impulsion as the transition is made. When first starting to concentrate on transitions, these should not follow too rapidly upon each other. Time must be allowed for the horse to become completely settled in the new pace, possibly for ten to twenty circles, before demanding another change. A youngster soon becomes mentally confused if this stage is hurried.

Transitions to a faster pace should be freely performed when demanded but more time must be allowed and some warning given when asking for a walk or halt. In neither case should the tension on the lunge rein be abandoned or increased but, for transitions to a slower pace, if the command proves insufficient, several short jerks in a downwards direction, causing the noseband of the cavesson to bump the front of the horse's nose, emphasise the demand. At the same time, the impulsion must be maintained to keep the horse in contact with the bit and to maintain the purity of the pace until the transition is achieved. The importance of all transitions 'going through' the horse, with the energy created by the hindquarters travelling through the suppleness of the horse, until it is accepted in the mouth, is a preparation for mounted work.

When asking the horse to halt, the same forward thinking must always apply, otherwise the horse, particularly a youngster, will sprawl on his forehand with his head up and very little weight on his hind legs. From this position it is almost impossible to restart in walk without first losing the correct rhythm. As, in the end, most horses are only too delighted to come to the halt, great skill is required with the whip to maintain the impulsion until the horse stands still. Even then, at least with older horses, the horse should be 'between the aids' and attentive to the trainer. Once halted, no horse should be allowed to turn into the circle or be drawn by the rein towards the trainer. At first, it may be necessary to raise the whip and point it towards the shoulder to discourage this habit, which is all too easily acquired and can become dangerous, especially with young colts who may strike with the forelegs when sent back with the whip.

The great value of correctly executed transitions is that they require a momentary increase of impulsion and great suppleness from tail to head. This suppleness is on a different plane from the lateral bend required to maintain the line of the circle, and so correct transitions are an added source of suppleness and the first steps towards collection.

Careful, progressive practice gradually enables the time between the command and the response to become shorter until, without loss of the rhythm or purity of the pace, the transition becomes 'direct', that is, with no intermediate steps in the change from one pace to another. Even before this stage is confirmed, a change in the whole outline of the horse may be noticed. There will be an overall picture of roundness rather than length.

Shortening the Side-reins

As the paces improve and the strides lengthen, the hind legs of the horse are brought further under the weight of his body, allowing the shoulders greater freedom and the head and neck to rise. The whole outline appears shorter and rounder and the side-reins begin to be too long for the horse to make contact with the bit, as he did in the early days of his training (Figure 17).

Figure 17   Horse beginning to collect itself and 'asking' for the side-reins to be shortened

When the trainer is sure that this stage has been reached, it is time to shorten the side-reins but only by the degree dictated by the horse's more advanced posture. In this way, the horse may be said to come up 'with the bit' and can constantly rely on it being still and easily within his reach. He has by now learned to accept it and, on any sudden loss of contact, should immediately begin to seek it. If he has to resort to his early long, low head carriage to make contact, his newly achieved balance and posture will either be displaced or he will cease to seek the bit and may well begin to toss and play with it. This gradual shortening of the side-reins to match the balance and outline of the horse is of immense importance and must never be anticipated or dictated by the trainer. The time it will take and the degree of shortening necessary is related to the fitness and conformation of each horse, but, with a well made horse, it may be necessary to take in two or three holes in the first instance and one or two later on in his training. At all times, the side-reins should be detached unless the horse is actually working and, in any case, should be longer or not used at all during the walk, unless it is of very short duration. The walk, with its four-time sequence and very little natural impulsion, is all too easily spoilt.

If, during this stage, any general stiffness or resistance in the mouth is noticed, the side-reins must be lengthened and the horse encouraged to regain his more novice outline until relaxation and suppleness returns. In any case, it is often wiser to 'work in' in this manner, if the horse has not been allowed to warm up without side-reins. All things being equal, should a young horse seem unhappy or unwilling to make contact with the bit, teething troubles should be suspected. You can sometimes ease this problem by using a rubber snaffle until the new teeth are through.

The Medium Trot

Until now, the horse has been in walk or working trot but once a good, even pace with a degree of elevation has been established, a start may be made towards a medium trot. This must be carried out as the working trot but with more impulsion and greater suspension. This allows time for the lengthening of the horse's stride without loss of balance. If the trainer tries to create a medium trot by increasing the speed of the working trot, the horse will either fall onto his forehand and take small running steps or throw up his head, hollow his back and only extend the forelegs. It is, therefore, essential that it is the impulsion and spring in the working trot which is increased to produce the medium trot.

If you attempt the working trot still on the circle, the chances of a young horse losing his balance are very great so it is probably wiser to drive him out of the circle onto a straight line for a few steps at a time, returning to the circle on a slightly different radius (Figure 18). In this way, the trainer can be sure that the working trot is good with sufficient energy to assist the horse to spring forward into a medium trot when allowed to leave the circle. The very fact that he is making a change of direction will encourage the horse to go freely forward and to take a few lengthened strides (Figure 19). He should then be brought

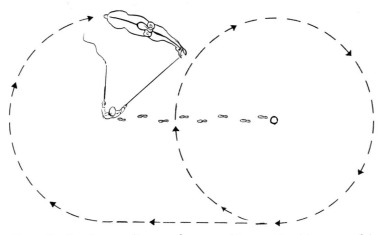

Figure 18 Creating a medium trot from a working trot, by driving out of the circle and returning on a different radius

back onto the circle and will instinctively correct his balance returning to the rounder, shorter step required for the working trot. By this method, not only does he learn to lengthen his stride but also to make smooth transitions from one trot to the other and back again.

During the medium trot, the horse's outline again becomes slightly longer and lower with the nose beyond the vertical, but the quarters are lower and the hind legs show much more energy than at the novice stage of training. At all times, the back must be rounded and supple with the tail gently swinging from side to side. Any tenseness in the back or mouth manifests itself in an artificial extension of the forelegs, with the heel of the fore feet making contact with the ground

Figure 19 Horse lengthening its stride as it goes off the circle

41

before the toe (Figure 20). This should never be accepted and is often a sign of hurried training and, once again, the only safe remedy is to return to the novice stage of training. Never forget that all paces must be and look natural.

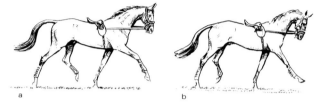

Figure 20   (a) The medium trot, showing natural, correct extension with the diagonals equidistant and the toe hitting the ground before the heel

(b) False extension with the heel of the fore feet hitting the ground before the toe

The Canter

It may well be that the horse's control and balance has been sufficiently established to allow him to canter on the circle before he is ready to attempt a few steps of medium trot. Nevertheless, it is often wiser to stick to the first order of training. If the horse is encouraged to canter on, it may well be difficult to stop him making this transition in favour of the extra effort needed to go into medium trot. Thus mental confusion or, worse still, evasions arise.

A canter is an easy pace for a horse, partly because the three-time rhythm seems better suited to the rhythm of his breathing than does the rhythm of the trot. Much research has yet to be done on this but it is a fact that, in the wild, the horse uses a walk or canter more frequently than the trot. In countries where the working horse covers long distances, eg herding cattle, this is mostly done at these paces. This may be the result of man seeking greater comfort for himself but unnoticed physiological reasons in the horse may also have played their part in developing this habit.

A horse on the lunge will nearly always go freely into a canter but, like the walk, this pace can lose its sequence very easily, so should not be introduced until the balance and impulsion is such that the horse can travel freely forward in a three-time working canter and still remain on the track of the circle. To do this, it is necessary for the quarters to be slightly lowered so that the hind legs can be brought sufficiently under the weight of his body for the forehand to be lightened and raised. As in the trot, the inside hind leg should come forward and slightly under the body and in line with the circle. This helps to transfer a good deal of the horse's weight towards the outside shoulder and gives more freedom to the leading inside leg. Again, the horse will use his head and neck as a balancing pole and turn slightly away and inwards towards the leading leg, thus producing a slight muscular bend throughout his whole length, which helps him to negotiate the circle despite the lack of lateral flexion in his spine. Once again, in bending his head and neck to the inside of the circle, he will make more contact with the outer side-rein and so accustom himself to the passive, outside rein which plays such a part in mounted canter work.

If the horse does not go freely forward in canter, he may not have confidence in the going, or the side-reins may be too short. It is often wise to dispense with these at first, provided that the trainer is in control. Any tendency to draw back and fall into a stiff-backed, four-time canter must be immediately discouraged, by use of the whip if necessary, as this breakdown in the sequence of the pace all too easily becomes a habit which will inhibit all future training when mounted.

Some trainers find that, when watching a horse working at fast paces, particularly in enclosed places, they become giddy. One cure is to watch the horse's tail for a circle or two because this swings across, and not with, the line of the circle. This often seems to correct the trouble and, in any case, the problem is usually forgotten when the trainer becomes more experienced.

6 WORK WITH CAVALETTI

Young horses can be introduced to cavaletti work on the lunge at quite an early stage in training. It is of great assistance in teaching the horse to relax and lower its head and neck, in helping to improve paces and also as a remedy against boredom. The trainer needs to be very well versed in the use of cavaletti because a mistake or an incorrect distance between the poles can have disastrous and long-lasting effects.

Both the side-reins and those belonging to the bridle should be removed when working over poles, for at no time should the horse connect jumping with a jerk in the mouth from the bit and this can easily happen if he becomes unbalanced and throws up his head.

Some trainers lunge over poles on the circle with the ends in the centre more closely placed than the outer (Figure 21). This allows the trainer to guide the horse over the poles at the exact distance most suited to his stride. Unfortunately, should a pole get displaced by a knock from the horse's hoof, the whole sequence will be wrong and the horse will have to be brought to an abrupt halt if he is not to transverse them again in this false position. It is, therefore, best to start by placing one thick, heavy pole on the ground in various parts of the school. During the lunge lesson on the circle bring the horse quietly to the walk, detach the side-reins, and lead him over the poles from every direction. For some reason, most horses are extremely suspicious of poles lying on the ground and should never be bustled over them. It is often helpful to allow them to stop and thoroughly sniff the poles before asking them to cross them. A clever trainer will not turn and look at his horse but will walk near his head and precede the horse over the pole.

Time spent on the first introduction to cavaletti work always pays dividends later. Once the horse has accepted that poles hold no danger for him, the number of consecutive poles can gradually be increased. The horse can be led down them occasionally, but always remember that, because of the sequence of steps in the walk, he can not manage more than three without breaking the rhythm of his pace.

Except for very small ponies, the distance between the poles should be 4–4½ft for both walking and trotting. It is essential that this distance is strictly maintained at all times and the advantage of having several lines of poles placed in various parts of the school is that, should they become displaced, they can be disregarded. If only one set is used, it is necessary to have an assistant to correct them and his very presence would be a distraction to both horse and trainer.

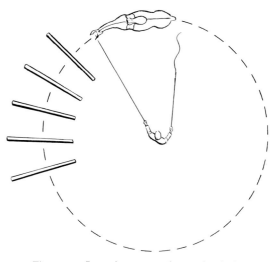

Figure 21   Lungeing over poles on the circle

Few horses take more than a day or so to get used to walking over poles and can soon be lunged over them at a trot. As in the case of the medium trot, they can be driven quietly out of the circle, onto a straight line, over three or four poles, and quietly back onto a circle in a different place. The trainer moves with the horse with long, even steps and keeps him between the rein and the whip though both of these should be as passive as possible. It is important for his future as a jumper that the horse learns to go forward over the poles at his own volition and not because of fear of the whip.

Clearly, calmness at all times is essential and the working trot on the circle must be soft and well defined before the horse is allowed to go on a straight line and over the poles. If the distance is right, the horse will be able to negotiate the poles without change of stride or rhythm, and should continue onto the next circle in the same way. If the distance is too great, the rhythm will be lost and the horse will begin to reach forward with the forelegs, with a high head carriage and a stiff, flat back. On the other hand, if it is too short, the pace will be checked and he will probably stumble over the poles and lose his confidence.

It is generally accepted that the initial introduction to trotting over poles should be done by allowing the horse to walk over the first three then encouraging him by the voice to trot on over the remainder. In this way, he is given time to assess his stride. For this reason, throughout all work using cavaletti or placing poles, the horse should always be allowed to come into the first pole at a walk or trot. Once the horse has become used to trotting down a line of four or five poles and quietly returning to the circle, they can be of immense value to his training, both on the flat and over jumps.

It is natural for the horse to lower his head and neck to look at the poles (Figure 22) this, in turn, rounds the long muscles over the back

Figure 22 Looking at the poles, a horse lowers its head and neck, a move which rounds the long muscles over the back

and loins and allows greater freedom for the hind legs to come under the weight of the body, while the need to lift the legs over the poles requires greater flexibility and, therefore, suspension.

Should the trot on the circle lose definition or suppleness, or the horse become inattentive, he can be driven once or twice down the line of poles to help correct the fault.

At this stage, it is not recommended that the poles should be raised above the ground and the use of cavaletti with cross-members at each end is strongly discouraged at all times. It is all too easy for them to roll along in front of the horse's hind feet and many serious accidents have occurred for this very reason. On the other hand, should a horse trip or fall over poles lying on the ground, very little harm occurs and, provided that his head is not restrained, the balance will soon be retrieved and the pace picked up again.

Lungeing Over Jumps

Once a horse has become accustomed to trotting down a line of four to six poles on the ground, there is always a risk that he may no longer treat them with respect. He may begin to go over them as a routine exercise without lowering his head to look at them and, eventually, without elevation or suppleness. This is, of course, basically the fault of the trainer in allowing boredom to set in by over-use of trotting poles. However, it is also the time to start training the horse to jump as this sort of calmness is all important at this stage.

The trotting stride of the average horse is about $4\frac{1}{2}$ft and that of the canter about double, ie 9ft. The first introduction to jumping is done by first allowing the horse to trot calmly down five to six poles on the ground. Then get an assistant to set up one end of the final pole on a block of wood or a five-gallon oil drum, to bring the penultimate pole up to this and to set the opposite end on another drum. In this way, three or four poles are left at trotting distance, followed by a gap of 9ft to the crossed poles (Figure 23). This allows the horse first to establish his balance and rhythm, take one stride of trot or canter, if he wishes, and then jump over the crossed poles. In actual fact, his first efforts are more likely to be an elevated canter stride than a marked jump but, as a jump is always in canter sequence, this is exactly what is required. The important point is that, as with the trotting poles, the horse must not be hurried or forced to jump by the use of the lunge whip but must go quietly forward down the poles and create the necessary extra impulsion required to negotiate the final obstacle at his own volition.

In this way, the horse learns to develop his abilities as a natural gymnast, always capable of judging the amount of effort required for each combination and distance, and of carrying out his work in a relaxed and supple manner, whatever the size of the fence. The foundations for this are laid the first time he is asked to trot down a line of poles on the ground. If he is driven out of the rhythm of the pace which has been established on the circle, calmness may be lost and his natural judgement and jumping ability may never be realized. The whole value of work over cavaletti, whether on the lunge or ridden, is that it develops the intelligence and agility of the horse without stress or strain. It cannot be over-emphasised how important

Figure 23 Establishing balance and rhythm as an introduction to jumping

it is that the distances between the poles or jumps are always exactly right for each horse, as nothing will destroy his confidence quicker than being 'wrong footed' at this stage of his training. The shortening and lengthening of stride in front of fences, which is required for cross-country or competitive jumping, should not be attempted until the horse's powers of collection are much more advanced and, in any case, this is probably better taught when mounted.

Once the horse has learned to trot quietly down the poles and to negotiate the crossed poles, these may be raised to form a very small parallel bar exactly 9ft away from the last trotting pole. The horse should be allowed to come down to this as previously and be left to sort out the difference for himself. It is of no great importance if he hits them, providing they are heavy and free to fall. Should he do so, return to the circle and re-establish the balance of his working trot, and his calmness, before allowing him to go down the poles again. In all probability, he will overdo the jump and may well put in a buck the other side. If this becomes a habit, it can usually be stopped by placing a further pole on the ground about 9ft the other side of the obstacle. Always bring the horse back onto a circle after going down a line of poles, partly for the trainer to regain control but also to ensure that the rhythm and suppleness of the trot is not lost. As stated earlier, at no time should the horse be allowed to come into the cavaletti at a canter but, later in his training, the walk can be the initial pace.

As the object of all jumping training is to teach the horse to jump in a natural style with a softly rounded back, most trainers use parallel bars to increase the size of the obstacle rather than upright fences, which make much greater demands on a young horse. Care must be taken, however, that the distance between the parallels is never so great that the horse can mistake them for trotting poles and try to jump 'in and out'.

Once the single fence has been mastered, a second obstacle can be inserted 9ft away from the first and 18ft beyond the last of the poles on the ground. When driven down this, the horse will make his usual jump over the first obstacle and land in canter at exactly the right distance to spring straight over the next fence. Once he has experienced this combination, he will begin to bring himself into the first trotting pole with sufficient impulsion to take him through the whole exercise. So he begins to learn to assess and adjust to each new task.

If they have never been hurried or frightened over cavaletti work, horses soon become almost fascinated by it and it requires considerable ingenuity on the part of the trainer to concoct suitable combinations commensurate with this stage of training. There are, of course, endless variations of combinations but, for the most part, they have no place in this book, as the limiting factor of cavaletti work on the lunge is the distance the trainer can move without actually running beside the horse while he negotiates the poles.

The trainer should always bear in mind that his task is to ensure that the horse's introduction to jumping is correctly and calmly carried out. By retaining only one pole on the ground as a placing pole and by inserting either a third small fence 9ft away, or by bringing the distance between the first two to 18ft, the horse can be made first to jump in and out (sometimes referred to as a canter line), or to take one non-jumping stride before clearing the final fence. This overall distance of approximately 27½ft is probably the maximum suitable for lunge work. As the horse progresses in his general work, you will be able to lunge him over a single fence but this must still have a placing rail, either on the ground or slightly raised, 9 or 18ft away from the fence. This stage is probably better left until the horse has achieved a more advanced stage of balance and collection. Once upright posts are used to hold the fence, it is wise to place a smooth pole from the top to the ground, in the form of a wing, to prevent the lunge rein catching on the upright.

At no time should horses be lunged consistently over fences but it can be part of their daily work from an early stage, if it is related to their work on the flat.

7 EVASIONS

However carefully one works and however much thought one gives to the training of a horse on the lunge, at some stage one is almost certain to have to contend with some form of evasion or resistance. In fact, a horse that never rebels is either very cold blooded and unintelligent, completely cowed or, more likely, not really being asked to work.

There are usually three basic causes of resistance: mental confusion, physical difficulties, or the loss of the initiative by the trainer. The first is probably the easiest to cure and is most often the result of muddled thinking and inconsistent commands from the trainer. One of the most common examples of this is the horse who refuses to stop, even at the walk, and continues to revolve in a dull, routine pace, despite all the trainer's efforts to bring him to the halt. In fact, the more the voice is raised and the lunge rein jerked, the more bemused the animal appears, almost as though it is autistic. If the pace is a canter, it is sometimes wise to wait passively until the horse 'runs down' but at a trot or walk work the circles towards the nearest wall or high hedge and then walk straight towards it, driving the horse out of the circle and into the wall, at the same time giving the firm command 'halt' (Figure 24). Of course, in the case of a hedge or fence, this must be high enough to be unjumpable and it is important that the horse is kept between the whip and the rein all the time, otherwise he can turn away and run down the wall or try to push past his trainer. Once the horse has come to the halt, the trainer should stand for a few seconds with the point of the whip raised towards him and then reverse it and, tucking the stock under his arm, walk quietly up to the horse and make a fuss of him.

In this way, the horse connects the command 'halt' first, with stopping on the circle, secondly, with not being allowed to turn in and, finally, with a reward. This will be the first form of discipline he will learn when mounted, ie to stop on command and to stand still.

The first physical resistances a trainer is likely to meet are either the horse trying to cut the corners or leaning hard on the lunge rein and trying to pull away from the circle. Both stem from the horse's natural preference to either the right or left side, from muscular

Figure 24 Curing a horse which refuses to stop, by walking it straight at a wall then giving the firm command, 'halt'

stiffness and the inherent rigidity of his spine. Much of how to deal with this has been covered in earlier chapters but until a horse is both fit and supple these troubles will continue to manifest themselves in various ways. Frequently, the horse which tries to cut corners is not truly between the rein and the whip, because the trainer has allowed himself to turn slightly faster than the horse, whose head is now in line with the trainer's shoulder instead of just beyond it. At the same time, the horse will be falling onto the inside shoulder, because the trainer is not concentrating on the inside hind leg and has allowed the pace and balance to deteriorate. It may also be caused by the circle being too small for the horse's stage of training. You can encourage the horse to make a true circle by enlarging the circle and lightening the tension on the lunge rein, at the same time, bringing the whip forward and pointing it at his shoulder (Figure 25). This allows the quarters to come inside the line of the circle, making it easier for him to bring the inside hind leg slightly under the body and to transfer more weight onto the outside shoulder. This position must be accepted until the horse is sufficiently supple to adjust his balance to the line of the circle. However, it should not be allowed to become a habit or the horse will never become truly 'straight'.

The same principles apply when the horse pulls out of the circle, only this time it is the quarters which must be driven out to encourage the horse to put more weight on his inside shoulder. You cannot do this by pulling the horse's head towards the inside or by reducing the circle, both of which will only destroy his balance to an even greater degree. In fact, it is better to lighten the tension on the lunge rein so that he gains no support from it and must establish his own balance.

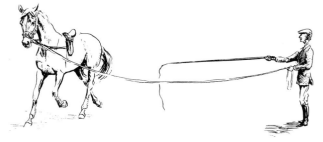

Figure 25   Encouraging a horse which falls in on the circle by bringing the whip forward and pointing it at the shoulder

Then, providing the horse is sent well forward in a good working trot, he will begin to make contact with the outside side-rein and to describe a correct circle with even tension on the lunge rein. Always remember that, whenever resistance springs from physical causes, it is wise to revert for a while to the horse's initial training with long side-reins and a long, low posture. However, if the horse is very strong and heavy and the trainer a light-weight, it is probably wiser to fit the cavesson as a drop-noseband and it may be necessary to shorten the inside side-rein for a few minutes to help send the quarters out until the trainer has control. However, this method should only be resorted to *in extremis* and should be dispensed with if the horse can be lunged in the corner of a school or around motor tyres, which make excellent markers. Nevertheless, if the horse's introduction to lunge work has not been hurried, neither method should be necessary.

Similarly, you should not have any problem with resistance in the back and mouth but, if for any reason you do, it is of no value to try and correct this fault by altering the height of the side-reins on the girth or roller. If the reins are made lower, the horse will tend to raise his head still further and, if they are raised, he will become more over-bent. As has been stressed all along, at no time should the reins be used to position the horse's head and neck, only to allow him to make contact with the bit.

Horses that are over-lunged or kept on the same rein and pace for long periods frequently devise tricks to escape the monotony, which in itself is a condemnation of the trainer's lack of intelligence and inventiveness. It often starts with the horse's realisation that, if he adopts a low head carriage and a lazy pace, he will be rewarded by being taken back to his stable. In truth, he is gradually creeping behind the aids and storing up his energy for further evasions. The trainer should recognise the difference between the horse which is really going forward with supple and unhurried strides and the one whose paces are routine and lacking in spring or energy.

Once the horse has learned to get 'behind the aids' the trainer is no longer his master and it is all too easy for him to escape from the circle in one way or another. Trouble usually starts by the horse stopping and swinging round to face the trainer (Figure 26a), who is immediately placed at a disadvantage because, if he walks towards the horse, it may well run backwards or turn across the rein and start revolving the other way round the circle. This latter frequently happens if the horse is very stiff on one rein. In both cases, the horse must be stopped but it is no use trying to pull him up with the lunge rein. Should the horse run back, the most effective deterrent is to run as fast as possible towards him, so giving him nothing to pull against (Figure 26b). He will almost certainly stop and can be approached carefully and led back onto the circle and restarted in work at the place where the disobedience first occurred. If, however, he turns onto the other circle, the trainer needs quickly to reverse the aids and probably the best way to do this is to reverse the whip and tuck the stock under the arm, at the same time taking up at least some of the lunge rein in what had been the whip hand. If the trainer is not very expert in the use of the whip, it is probably wiser to drop it as soon as trouble starts as a wildly waving whip only adds to the confusion and the horse, anticipating punishment, may become very hard to

Figure 26 (a) A bored or crafty horse which has mastered the aids will cause trouble by swinging round to face the trainer

(b) Counteract this by running towards the horse as fast as possible, giving it nothing to pull against

(c) Having dropped the whip, bring the horse to you by means of the voice

control. Once the aids, are changed, the horse can be brought to a halt by the use of the voice (Figure 26c) or, if necessary, by driving him into the wall. He must then be lead back onto the correct circle and the work recommenced from the same spot where the trouble first started. This time, make sure that he is between the aids and really working.

These troubles often occur each time the horse passes the same part of the circle and a clever trainer must anticipate them and, if the habit has become really confirmed, attempt to frustrate the horse by asking for greater impulsion just before reaching the trouble spot. Usually, the difficult spot is the place nearest to the direction of the stables or the door. One solution is to lunge as close to the gate or door as reasonable, because it is only possible really to control a disobedient horse on the circle, once he is allowed to get going in a straight line very few men can stop him. This is particularly the case when, instead of turning into the circle, the horse swings his quarters towards the trainer and runs straight out of the circle. Then the trainer's only hope is to drop the whip and, by bending his knees and leaning back against the rein, rely on his dead weight and the use of the voice to bring the horse to a stop (Figure 27). He will not be able to do this unless his

Figure 27 Stop a disobedient horse from running off in a straight line by dropping the whip, bending the knees and leaning back against the reins. If all else fails – see insert – run the lunge-rein through the inside snaffle ring, over the head and fasten to the outside ring to create a successful gag

initial position has been correct and this is why such emphasis was put on this in Chapter 3. If this fails, and it often does, the tension on the lunge rein should be abandoned by once more running as fast as possible in the same direction as the horse, once again relying on the sudden loss of support and the trainer's voice at least to slow the horse down. If, however, he is too strong and gets beyond recall, the only safe thing is to abandon the rein and let him go, otherwise the trainer may well fall and be dragged, which can be very dangerous. Some older horses become very adept at escaping by this method and the only safe way to forestall them is by erecting barriers and to commence work on the rein on which such disobedience is less likely to happen. You will find that this is usually the stiff side since it is sometimes more difficult for the horse to swing his quarters in on that side.

A more subtle form of disobedience is found in the horse who anticipates the trainer's commands. Although this denotes attention and intelligence, it takes the prerogative away from the trainer and should be stopped. It is the trainer who should always dictate the pace, particularly in transitions, when it is so important that the horse always goes truly forward and does not just drop back into a slower pace or just gradually pick up speed when changing into trot or canter.

Troubles start for many reasons but nearly all are contributable to lack of skill or concentration on the part of the trainer. It is vital, therefore, that there should not be any form of distraction while lungeing, with the possible exception of music.

If all else fails, rather than allowing a young horse to learn that he is so much stronger than his trainer, it may be wise to abandon the principle that he should never be lunged with the rein attached to the bit. By running the lunge rein through the inside snaffle ring and over his head and fastening it to the outside ring, a very successful gag is created which can be brought into action by just increasing the tension on the lunge line. This acts on the corners of the mouth so does not damage the bars and, by causing the horse to raise his head sharply, is a very efficient check on an impetuous or disobedient horse. However, this method should not be resorted to by inexperienced trainers and, in any case, only as a method of control when other methods have failed. The danger is that, all too easily, it can destroy the horse's wish to go forward to seek the bit and can also teach him to get behind it. Nevertheless, some very experienced trainers always use the lunge rein in this manner from the earliest lessons, but their timing and co-ordination has to be of the highest degree to achieve real success.

8 FURTHER TRAINING

Deliberately, no timetable has been given with this book as this must vary with every horse, but at all times, lungeing may be carried out in conjunction with mounted training. A horse may be backed as soon as it is capable of being lunged quietly and understands the use of the voice, and this gradual integration should continue throughout the horse's life. Even an advanced horse may develop some form of stiffness or suffer an injury which makes it impossible for it to be ridden for a while, in which case, lungeing may be the answer. Alternatively, some mental confusion may arise which may easily be dispersed by a quiet session on the lunge. Certainly, a horse that has been out of work for any length of time should always be lunged before coming into work under saddle. It is probably safe to suggest that, whenever you intend to take a horse a step further in his training, it should first be taught on the lunge. This particularly applies to gradual collection in the paces, training for which should have been started earlier through the transitions and the horse's need to gather himself together when jumping.

Slowly the muscular fitness, impulsion and balance of the horse has been improved and become established. The quarters should now be lower and the forehand light with the head and neck higher and the face nearly vertical to the ground. Once again, the side-reins will appear too long and need to be shortened one or two holes. The whole outline of the horse should now appear rounder and the base shorter. Nevertheless, if the horse has been properly taught, he should not have lost the habit of immediately relaxing and returning to a more novice outline whenever the side-reins are lengthened or removed. In other words, he should never cease to seek the bit. If this happens, he is not truly going forward and the trainer should go to bed in tears!

Once the horse is approaching this more advanced outline, he may be worked on a smaller circle in both trot and canter, but not in the walk when he must always be encouraged to have as free and long a stride as possible. The truly collected walk is one of the last movements to be mastered and is probably better done from the saddle.

A very good exercise to help collection is gradually to reduce the size of the circle while asking for a little more impulsion, and then to allow the horse to go out again in ever-increasing circles until he reaches the original line, without losing the collection that he achieved on the smaller circle. Care must be taken never to reduce the circle beyond the horse's current capabilities, otherwise stiffness and loss of rhythm will result. At all times the degree of collection asked must be dictated by the horse's ability and must never be attempted by force. At this stage it should be possible to ask for direct transitions from one pace to the next and to begin to expect the horse to go from walk to canter and back to walk, and from trot to halt without any intermediate steps. When halted, the horse should be encouraged to stand square with his weight evenly distributed over all four legs and, even when stationary, to have enough inherent impulsion to move off immediately on command.

Once a fair degree of collection has been established in both canter and trot, some extension may be attempted and this is best taught in the same way as was used for the medium trot earlier in his training. That is by first ensuring that the collected pace in the circle is both supple and active and then driving the horse out of the circle and into extension for a few paces, before returning to the collected pace again on another circle. It is rather reminiscent of the uncoiling and rewinding of a spring and must never be forced but be the result of the greater activity and elevation in the collected pace, giving time for the horse really to lengthen his stride when allowed to go in a straight line. It should never be forgotten that all paces must be and appear natural and, if the collection is insufficient or artificial, the extension will be false and done with a flat back and exaggerated foreleg action. If this happens, as always, the only remedy is to allow the horse to return to a less advanced outline and recommence his training from that stage.

A horse working at this standard may not need to be lunged at all, but to do so acts as an invaluable check by which the trainer can ensure that the horse's work under saddle has not destroyed the purity of his paces, that he moves in an equally relaxed and supple manner on both reins, and that the impulsion is really going through, particularly in transitions, and not being weakened through lack of 'straightness'. It is only on the lunge that the trainer is able to really study his horse visually. Although he may feel all is well when riding, he may get so accustomed to the horse's way of going that stiffness and/or lack of impulsion go undetected. Such delusions may comfort the rider but can have disastrous consequences for his mount. Concussion, sprains and arthritic complaints are all too often caused by a lack of suppleness and balance in the rider setting up a reciprocal stiffness and tension in the horse.

Once a horse has reached this stage, and it may well take three or four years, work on a circle assumes more the role of a way of 'warming-up' than a training exercise, because the next stage requires the horse to be worked in hand. For this method, the trainer is close to the horse's head but still holds a shorter lunge rein in his outside hand and a short whip in the other (Figure 28). The horse is brought into a

Figure 28 Work in hand: the *piaffe*

high degree of collection and the side-reins are shortened in relation to this. All work is now done in a straight line, with the trainer taking long strides beside the horse's shoulder. The horse can now, very gradually, be brought into advanced movements such as *piaffe* and *passage* and even later into work above the ground, such as *levade*, *courbette* and *capriole*. However, there are very few horses and even fewer men capable of reaching this stage and it should only be attempted after years of experience and expert tuition.

Probably, only when the abilities of horse and trainer have reached this expert level, should lungeing become an end in itself, rather than a means to an end. Nevertheless, it can be a boundless source of interest and pleasure demanding, as it does, great powers of concentration, knowledge and self-control. It also requires dexterity, quick wits and, above all, a love and understanding of all types of horses. Provided that they always make haste slowly, it is well within the compass of most horsemen.

PART TWO

LUNGEING THE RIDER

9 THE ROLE OF THE LUNGE HORSE

The value of riding without stirrups on a lunge horse has long been appreciated on the Continent. Most children and beginners are introduced to riding in this way and experienced riders and, in particular, those at the Spanish Riding School constantly use this method to check their position and relaxation. This practice is slowly being adopted in Britain and many people now appreciate its great value for all riders and, ultimately, for their mounts too. We are still sadly handicapped, however, by the lack of well trained horses and competent instructors for it is not enough that they should know how to work a horse on a circle. Without the knowledge and understanding of the correct training of the horse on the lunge, many instructors are unable to anticipate and prevent the difficulties and evasions which can so quickly occur. On the other hand, those who are talented trainers from the ground, all too often, lack the necessary experience of mounted work to enable them to help other riders.

This is a sorry state of affairs because, undoubtedly, some of the best horses in the world are bred in Britain. There are, also, untold numbers of dedicated riders, yet few reach their true potential because few horses are correctly broken or receive sufficient basic training, while their riders dissipate the energy of their mounts and themselves by never establishing a correct position in the saddle. Both these failings can be overcome by working horses and humans on the lunge.

So far, the emphasis has been on the careful training or re-training of horses. When considering the use of the lunge to help train riders a slightly different principle must apply. The trainer now becomes an instructor and the horse must be subservient to the rider's needs. Obviously, young horses or those intended for advanced training should never be used for this work. Yet a good lunge horse is a specialist in his own right and should be highly valued. He should have been just as slowly and carefully introduced to lunge work as any other horse and have shown an aptitude for it. As he will be ridden by many different riders the lunge horse must have substance without losing quality. His movement should be free and, although he must be able to lengthen his stride, a soft, rather rounded action is usually easier for the rider who may get left behind the movement on a strong, long-striding animal (Figure 29).

Figure 29 The lunge horse

Natural balance and a well sloping shoulder not only give the pupil an easier ride but help to instil confidence in novice riders. The horse must be straight, ie the hind feet must follow in the tracks of the fore feet while on the circle, otherwise the tension and crookedness in his spine will affect the rider's position and set up reciprocal stiffness. Many short–coupled horses with well sprung ribs make excellent lunge horses but care must be taken that they maintain their suppleness otherwise the novice rider may not be able to relax when working in trot.

Above all else, the lunge horse must have a really calm temperament and willingly go on working whatever is happening on his back. He must respect the whip but not react in any sudden way should it be used. He also needs to be very attentive to the instructor's voice as, contrary to the advice given for training a horse on the lunge, there will be a lot of extraneous noise and he must be able to recognise which commands are intended for him rather than the rider.

No horse under six years should be used for this work as it is very demanding. Unsound horses, even though not actually lame, should never be used as constant work on the circle carrying an often un-stable weight would inevitably aggravate the trouble. Equally, horses with poor conformation, such as weak hocks and close action, are likely to damage themselves even when wearing boots or bandages.

Needless to say it takes a skilful trainer to prevent a horse from becoming thoroughly stale with this work and every effort should be made to give lunge horses a change of activity and environment. In any case, a lesson should not last more than about fifteen minutes on each rein. This regular slow work keeps a horse muscularly fit but it should be remembered that respiratory troubles may result if fast work is only intermittent and that quiet hacking on a long rein is probably the best form of relaxation for horses that are used almost exclusively for lunge work.

Tack

A plain snaffle bridle and a lungeing cavesson should be fitted as described in Chapter 2 but, of course, the roller is replaced by a saddle. This should fit both the horse and the rider and, like all tack used for lungeing, should be soft and in first-class condition.

Particular care should be given to the girth straps and to the stitching of the buckles on the girth as they are subjected to great strain by the constant bend in the horse's ribs and the lack of steadiness in the rider. Reins may be left on the bridle although they are rarely used only, in this case, they should not be twisted and attached to the throat lash but knotted and left lying on the horse's neck. This tends to give confidence to nervous beginners and, in any case, they are then avail-able should the instructor ever lose contact with the lunge rein.

Most of the work will be done without stirrups but the bars on the saddle should be such that it is easy to take off or replace them without effort. Side-reins are essential and should be attached to the girth straps as described in Chapter 4 but care must be taken that they do not create a bulge under the rider's legs. They must not be attached to the rings of the snaffle unless the horse is actually working and should be undone if it is ever necessary to hold a long discussion with the pupil, or when both are resting. Otherwise, the horse may learn to play with the bit or become over-bent which is very disconcerting for the novice rider who can do nothing to correct this fault and may feel insecure with little head and neck in front of him.

Some riders are inclined to lose their position and to shift their weight onto different parts of the horse's back in which case it may be advisable to use a sheepskin numnah under the saddle. In any case, great care must always be taken of the horse's back. It should never be clipped out and the slightest swelling or localized sweating should be treated at once. Salt and water or a paste made of vinegar and whiting are often very effective if applied immediately and the horse is rested.

As always, boots or bandages should be fitted all round. Before the horse is in motion the side-reins should be connected to the rings of the snaffle and so adjusted that the horse is able to move freely forward without losing a fairly advanced outline: if the reins are too long he may fall on his forehand and so upset the rider's balance; if too short, he will inevitably retract his head and neck and hollow his back, much to his and the rider's discomfort. In other words, a horse used for the lungeing of riders must have been slowly and correctly trained to at least medium standard if he and the rider are not to suffer.

10 THE INSTRUCTOR

The whole object of lunge work for riders is to teach them firstly to adopt the correct position in the saddle and then to sit still in relation to the movement of the horse. Only when these two skills are truly mastered is it possible for the rider to control and direct his horse with effective but almost invisible aids. Only then will riding become an art rather than a form of exercise and only then will the horse have a chance to reach its full potential. It is this highly specialised relationship between man and his mount that separates the ordinary rider from the true horseman. Practice and dedication, together with an inborn sympathy and flair, are the essentials for the latter, but many who are quite content just to enjoy hacking about the countryside would find that work on the lunge could add greatly to their pleasure and to the safety of themselves and their horses.

It is essential that anyone who undertakes the instruction of a rider on the lunge should be in complete control of the horse and should ensure that all tack is correctly and securely fitted. If possible, the horse should be well used to the instructor's voice, and the words of command to him must always be consistent and completely different from those used to the rider. Ideally, the lesson should take place indoors for being in an enclosure tends to give confidence to novice or nervous riders and good going is ensured. However, if the use of an indoor school is not possible every effort should be made to produce a soft springy surface in a secluded place and to provide some form of barrier. Rough or slippery going will destroy the rider's and the instructor's concentration and can easily cause an accident or damage to the horse.

The instructor should insist that the rider wears a hard hat, which in the case of a cap should have a flexible peak. Breeches or jodphurs are also essential and should stirrups be used only boots or strong shoes with full-length soles and flat heels should be allowed. The safety factor should always be borne in mind as should the advisability of taking out some form of third party insurance.

Once again, it is essential that the instructor stands still and that the horse describes a true circle. Any tendency to lose the line or to cut corners immediately sets up problems for the rider and eventually causes stiffness in the horse.

With a well trained horse it may not be necessary to carry a whip but, if it is, it is usually wise to reverse it and place the stock under the arm which is not holding the lunge rein. In this position it can be brought quietly forward if necessary or dropped should any unforseen difficulties arise. Carried in this way, the thong trails behind the instructor and does not become entangled with his legs, and he can walk up to the rider without worrying the horse. A good lunge horse should react almost entirely to the instructor's voice but should it be necessary to use the whip the end of the lash should be quietly dropped just above the horse's inside hock. Skilfully done, this may not even be noticed by the rider. The instructor should adopt the correct posture for lungeing and, as his eyes should concentrate on the rider's position, must make sure that the horse is always slightly in front of his shoulder, as described in Chapter 3. If the horse is allowed to drop back 'behind the aids' the impulsion will be lost and it may be difficult for the rider to establish a sense of rhythm; nor must the horse be allowed to dictate the pace as it will be necessary, at least with novice riders, to adjust this to suit their ability and balance.

Finally, of course, any instructor undertaking such work must himself be highly qualified in the art of riding and have the ability to impart this knowledge in such a manner that the rider has absolute confidence in him at all times. Even advanced riders should feel able to leave the control of the horse solely to the instructor and so concentrate entirely on acquiring a supple, balanced position completely free of mental or physical tension.

Before starting a lesson it is wise to lunge the horse for a few minutes without side-reins to allow him to stretch his muscles, relax his back and get over any unwanted exuberance. Once he has blown his nose a few times and is moving freely it is generally safe for the rider to mount. The instructor should halt the horse on the circle and move out to him and stand in front of his head, while the rider mounts in the usual manner or receives a leg-up should the stirrups have been removed. There is no need to attach the side-reins at this stage, and the horse should be allowed to stand in a relaxed manner while the instructor ensures that the rider is sitting comfortably in the centre of the saddle and discusses the forthcoming lesson with him. Many instructors allow riders to retain their stirrups at this stage as the main object is to give confidence and to get them to relax, but the reins should be knotted and left lying on the horse's neck. If you want to retain stirrups on the saddle during the lesson, pull the buckle down about 4in from the bars and then simply cross the leathers over the front of the saddle (see Figure 30); in this way they will not rub the rider's thighs.

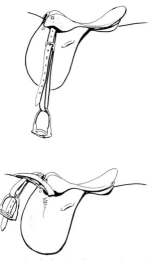

Figure 30 If stirrups are retained during lessons they should simply be crossed over in front of the saddle

For a complete beginner it may be necessary to use an assistant to lead the horse in the same way as the young horse was introduced to work on the circle. Such an assistant does not need a whip but should gradually work down the lunge rein towards the instructor as the rider's confidence grows. The assistant should not speak either to the horse or the rider, as both must be encouraged to concentrate on the instructor alone.

71

All early lessons should aim at, building up the rider's confidence; correction of his position should be left until some degree of relaxation is evident. To this end, the rider should be encouraged to hold the front of the saddle and to whistle or sing in time to the horse's rhythm, or should carry on a conversation with his instructor. Either method stops him holding his breath and building up extra tension. The experienced rider may not be nervous on the lunge but often finds it hard not to try and control the horse by using the aids. This must be discouraged as his whole concentration should be on his own position. All riders should be told to breathe slowly with a slight emphasis on exhalation to help relaxation.

Few lessons should exceed fifteen minutes on each rein including considerable rest periods when the rider is allowed to adopt any position he likes and to drop his toes again. During such periods, the horse should either be halted or quietly walking and, if possible, the side-reins should be unfastened and crossed over his neck. Never join them together or clip them to the saddle at this time as it could be possible for the rider's leg or hand to become entangled in the loop. This particularly applies when the rider is dismounting and can be very dangerous.

At the beginning of a lesson, all riders should be encouraged to slip their fingers under the front of the saddle and to use this to help maintain their balance. The wrist should remain supple and not be pressed against the leather as this tends to push the rider's seat backwards when the opposite is required. Instead, they should pull themselves gently forward until they are sitting in the centre and lowest part of the saddle with their legs hanging loosely down and the toes dropped. The object at this stage is to get as much of the rider's weight as possible over the horse's centre of gravity which lies just behind the withers.

11 THE CLASSICAL POSITION

The classical position is both natural and wholly logical. Untutored children riding bare-back on a pony inevitably finish up with most of their weight just behind the withers and, with dropped toes and rounded back, bring to mind the horsemen on the Parthenon Frieze. They have only to straighten the upper body and drop the heels slightly to come very close to the teaching of Xenophon, born circa 430 BC, or of any of the great masters of horsemanship who came after him (see Figure 31). To have withstood the test of time this position is clearly both simple and practical, at the same time, lending elegance and grace to horseman and mount, and thus warrants the appellation 'classical'.

Figure 31 An untutored child riding bareback, and his 'shadow' showing the slight readjustment necessary to achieve the classic position

The basic criterion for assessing the correct position is that an imaginary vertical line should pass from the rider's ear, through his

73

shoulder and hip-bone to his heel (see Figure 32). At the same time, a line dropped from the point of his knee should touch the toe of his boot. Only in this posture is his weight concentrated over the horse's centre of gravity.

Figure 32 The classic position showing an imaginary vertical line from the rider's ears through the shoulder and hip bone to the heel

Once the rider has pulled himself forward in the saddle and over this point the next step is to adopt an upright position. To achieve this he must be sufficiently relaxed and supple that by raising the waist or, as some trainers prefer to say, the diaphragm, his weight will be brought forward off the buttocks and onto the two seat bones and, to a certain extent, dispersed down the thighs. If this is done without force or tension the head will automatically rise, the shoulders and upper arms will drop and the spine will assume its natural curvature (Figure 33).

Throughout all work on the lunge, the rider should always look straight ahead between his horse's ears and be discouraged from looking either down or at his instructor. The human head is very heavy and can easily alter the rider's and, ultimately, the horse's balance.

From the beginning, a rider should be taught that, provided there is no tension, the elevation of his trunk and upper body is inter-related to the sense of gravity in his limbs. He should, as it were, feel the weight seeping out from the point of his elbows and knees and, finally, his heels.

Right from the start, riders must be discouraged from using any form of grip to maintain their position. It must only come from a secure and independent sense of balance. The lower on the saddle the knee is, the closer the rider gets to his horse's back and so, in effect, the tighter the overall contact becomes – rather like pushing a clothes peg down on a line. This is, in fact, a passive form of grip which is maintained by the rider's muscular reaction and relaxation being completely

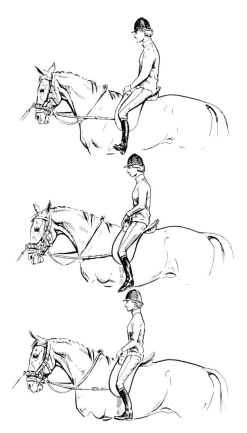

Figure 33 Rider adopting an upright position over the centre of balance

in harmony with that of his horse. Any conscious effort to hold this position, by contracting the muscles in the knees or thighs, has the opposite to the desired effect – it causes the rider either to push himself out of the saddle or to draw up his legs and so destroy the correct position.

Such a position is not possible unless the rider's inner thighs lie close to the saddle with as much as possible of surplus fat and muscle behind the thigh bone. Riders with rounded thighs will find this a handicap at first and are advised to swing both legs back and then slide them gently forward against the saddle.

It is possible to practice the classical position from the ground by standing with the feet slightly apart, the waist well up and the shoulders and elbows dropped while the hands hold imaginary reins. Looking straight forward it is then only necessary to bend the knees until their point is in line with the toe. Then the rider will find that he is standing in the position which is used for most forms of riding on the flat. By further closing the angles at the hips, knees and ankles the rider can assume the basic position for riding over fences or at the gallop.

Provided that the waist has not been allowed to collapse and the back is still straight, the imaginary line will now run vertically from the ear to the heel, but not through the hips which should now be behind this line. In both positions the centre of balance remains the same, ie directly over the horse's centre of gravity. Only in this position can there be complete synchronisation of the rider's movements and those of his horse at all times. Thus it becomes obvious there is really only one basic position which can be adapted to suit all forms of riding.

12 EXERCISES ON THE LUNGE

Correcting the Position

Once the rider has gained confidence and can adopt and maintain a reasonable position while the horse is quietly walking the time has come to demand more of him. First at the halt and then in the walk the rider should take hold of the arch of the saddle and, having checked that he is sitting in the deepest part of the saddle and that the body is upright and relaxed, he should stretch both legs away from the saddle and then allow them to fall gently back. This should be repeated several times and every effort made to lengthen the leg and so allow the knee to fall back into a lower position on the saddle (see Figure 34). At first the lower leg will tend to stick out, away from the horse's sides, and at this stage this is acceptable as, when the knee becomes more relaxed, this part of the leg will gradually make contact in the right place – that is to say, with the inner side of the calf muscles touching the horse just behind the girth. Any effort to make such contact before the whole leg, and, in particular, the thighs and knees are relaxed not only sets up tension but may cause the rider to turn the knee outwards, sit on his buttocks and grip with the backs of his calves.

One way to prevent this habit forming is to ask the rider to keep his feet as near as possible parallel to the horse's sides but again this depends to a great extent on the rider's conformation and his degree of suppleness, and can set up reciprocal stiffness if insisted upon in the early stages. It should become instinctive to riders of all standards to do this leg-stretching exercise before starting work either on or off the lunge.

Work in Sitting Trot

Most work on the lunge is done in trot as this has an easy two-time rhythm and the horse's action only displaces the rider on one vertical plane, unlike the canter which combines the upward thrust with a horizontal rocking movement. After the initial warming-up period, riders rarely use stirrups while on the lunge, so rising to the trot is of no value at this stage. This means that the rider must learn to accept all the movement of the horse's back. Few riders find this easy, mostly because they instinctively withdraw from it, instead of absorbing it through the supple muscles of the seat, loins and thighs.

The rider should try to feel the rhythm of the horse's paces and, without losing the correct position, sink softly down in the saddle as each set of diagonal legs touches the ground. In this way, both horse and rider will rebound together. Until this sense of joint harmony is

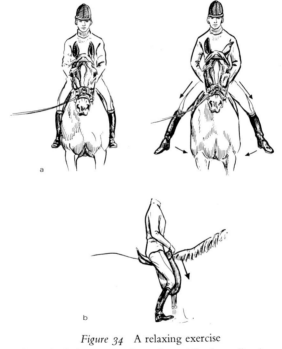

Figure 34 A relaxing exercise
(a) by stretching both legs away from the saddle then allowing them to fall gently back
(b) lengthening the leg with the knee falling back into a lower position on the saddle

established, neither will be able truly to relax or find his balance. Childish as it sounds, it may even help to get the rider to think that he is 'bouncing' the horse, not the other way round. As the rider's position improves, this synchronisation becomes instinctive and is one of the basic essentials if the rider is ever to be really skilled in the riding and training of horses.

It is understandable that all riders want to go out just to enjoy riding but, for the sake of themselves and their horses, they will find it is well worth working to achieve a classical position so that it becomes completely natural and they can automatically adopt it whatever saddle or horse they sit on. This may well take years to establish and even advanced riders need occasional checks and frequently to ride without stirrups even when not on the lunge. It would be fair to say that, although stirrups are necessary for jumping and some fast work, they are, more often than not, the cause of the average rider's poor position in the saddle because, so often, he relies on them and the reins to maintain his balance.

Changing Rein

Once the rider can sit comfortably to the trot for about five minutes the horse should be brought gently back to walk and then halted. The instructor, coiling the lunge rein as he goes and with his whip reversed, should walk out to the horse's head and allow the rider to relax for a few moments before changing onto the other rein. It is important that riders are viewed from both sides as, like horses, few people are equal sided and slim riders in particular are apt to twist in the saddle, forcing one leg forward and the other too far back. If this is corrected in isolation, ie by considering only one side, it can easily make matters worse on the other, unseen side. It is important constantly to change the rein and sometimes to have an assistant watching the other, outer side.

Twisting in the saddle is often the result of the rider trying to ride longer than his state of suppleness allows. This particularly applies when the muscles of the inner thighs are tense. It may also be due to the horse being too wide for a rider with narrow hips. A useful guide is that at all times the rider should have his hips and his shoulders parallel to those of his horse.

Another common fault which can often only be seen from outside the circle is turning out the toe and gripping with the back of the calf on that side (see Figure 35). This is usually accompanied by the rider tending to lean into the circle in an effort to counteract centrifugal force. This can be offset by making the circle larger and working at a slower pace until the position is more established.

Figure 35 A common fault, turning out the toe and gripping with the back of the calf

When actually putting the horse onto the other rein the instructor should walk round the horse and not pull his head towards the centre of the circle and push his quarters round. Having lead him round, the whip and rein can be quietly changed into the other hand, the whip still reversed and being passed behind the instructor's back if the horse is at all likely to react to it.

Further exercises

When the rider can maintain a reasonably good position on both reins, is supple and in harmony with his horse's paces, further exercises can be attempted. Until now, both hands have been on the arch of the saddle but the inside hand can now be removed and the arm allowed to hang down just behind the rider's thigh. The whole arm must be completely relaxed and may even swing slightly in time to the horse's movement. This is primarily to instil in the rider the importance of a completely relaxed upper arm when he ultimately holds the reins and, in the case of a beginner, it starts to give him confidence in his balance while in motion. Do not ask the rider to drop the outside arm as holding the saddle with the inside hand tends to make riders lean into the circle. It is therefore better to change the rein.

As soon as there is no noticeable difference in the rider's position on either rein he should be encouraged to let go of the saddle altogether and let both arms hang down just behind the thighs for two or three circuits. No exercise should be too prolonged; it is better to repeat it after frequent rest periods thus giving the rider a chance to hold the saddle and to check his position or to relax at the walk.

Once the rider has sufficient confidence, he can begin to hold 'imaginary reins', with the elbows bent so that, seen from the side, his forearm is in a straight line towards the horse's mouth and the hands could be said to be 'holding a book' with supple wrists and the thumbs uppermost. It is important to check that this is not achieved at the expense of relaxation in the upper arm or shoulders. Nor should the elbows stick out but just rest lightly on the point of the rider's hip. If this does not happen quite naturally it is almost invariably because the rider has collapsed at the waist and is sitting on his buttocks rather than his seat bones. If this is the case, as with the young or spoilt horse, it is better to return to the basic exercises, in the case of the rider, correcting the overall position rather than one part of the anatomy.

Rising to the Trot

Contrary to the usually accepted practice, it is often a good idea to wait until a beginner or an inexpert rider has mastered the basic position and can adjust his balance to his horse's paces without holding the saddle, before introducing or trying to improve the way he rises to the trot. At this stage of training, although he will have learned to pull himself forward and down onto the saddle he will not have come to rely on artificial means or the reins to help him rise. Also, he should be well used to the two-time rhythm of the horse's trot.

The stirrups are now re-attached to the saddle and so adjusted that, when the rider is sitting in the correct position with the knee as low on the saddle as is comparable to his stage of training, the ball of the foot rests lightly on the stirrup iron with the heel slightly dropped and the whole foot as parallel to the horse's sides as the rider's conformation allows. It is very important that the length of the leathers is dictated by the rider's position and not the other way round, although at first most riders tend to ride a little shorter with stirrups than without.

If the rider maintains his accustomed suppleness he has only to bring his upper body very slightly forward, and allow each alternate thrust of the horse's back just to lift his seat bones from the saddle, to be rising to the trot. This should be almost a mechanical operation instigated by the action of the horse and not the result of conscious effort on the part of the rider. If this is not so, he will probably jump into the air by straightening the knee and springing off the irons and/or by gripping. If this is the case, not only will suppleness be lost, but the lower legs will be seen to jerk away from the horse's sides in time to the trot. This has a soporific effect on the horse and also negates any hope of using light and almost invisible aids in the future. These faults often occur through the rider rising unnecessarily high or lifting his hands in time with his seat.

The supple rider with an established position and a balance entirely independent of his hands should only need to leave the saddle by an inch or so and let all the influence of his weight go forward and down his thighs. In this way, most of the movement is in the hip joint and not the knees, the legs stay still and close to the horse's side and the rider is able to return softly to the saddle. Meanwhile, his hands, still holding imaginary reins, remain still and unaffected by the movement in the rest of the rider's body. Now, the rider will be able to give correct and sympathetic aids when the reins become a reality.

Changing the Diagonals

As soon as the rider has mastered the rhythm and can rise smoothly to the trot he should be taught to distinguish between the two diagonals, preferably by feeling which pair of the horse's legs hit the ground as he sinks softly down into the saddle himself. If he finds this difficult, he should be encouraged to watch which shoulder goes forward as he rises and, by reversing this in his mind, he will know that his weight is coming down in time with that foreleg and the opposite hind leg. Provided that he rises with the outside foreleg and so sits as the inside hind leg comes to the ground, he is said to be riding on the outside diagonal, which is more-or-less standard practice when riding on a circle.

The rider should then be encouraged to remain sitting for one extra stride, so changing the diagonal, until he instinctively knows which one he is using. This is of great importance in the training of horses, and the use of the outside diagonal also relates to the way horses negotiate circles and bends despite the lack of lateral flexion in their spines (see page 31).

More Advanced Exercises

So far, all the work on the lunge has been to improve the rider's position and to give confidence. However, to ride well it is essential that the rider has complete control of all his muscular reactions as, unlike many other sports, he will often have to use parts of his body in isolation, ie apply greater emphasis to one aid then another, at the same time maintaining an overall stillness in relation to his horse. The following exercises will help towards this and should be carried out without stirrups at the walk and in trot. They should be done for short periods only and in rhythm to the horse's movements.

Holding the saddle, if necessary, the rider should first correct his position and then allow his neck muscles to relax, his head to hang forward and then roll it gently to each side until his chin rests lightly on his shoulder (see Figure 36). No force must be used to obtain this position, nor must the shoulders be raised to meet the chin, nor the back rounded. This exercise is particularly good for riders who tend to clench their teeth and ride with their jaw stuck forward as it makes them relax the muscles in the back of the neck. But this very common and ugly fault stems principly from a collapsed waist and tenseness in the shoulders and will usually disappear as the rider's position improves. For similar reasons, the rider should be asked to shrug his shoulders, to lift them up as high as possible and then allow them to drop back. This exercise must be carried out with the rest of the body in an upright position, otherwise the shoulders may not really drop back but only become rounded with the chest and even the waist collapsed.

Mental tension invariably seems to manifest itself in the back and shoulders and the following arm-swinging exercise will do much to disperse any stiffness in that area. Again, if necessary, the rider may

Figure 36 Relaxing exercises for neck muscles

hold the saddle with one hand and then, having dropped the other arm just behind the thigh, as in the earlier exercise, should swing the whole arm forward and up until the upper arm is just behind his ear when it should be allowed to drop back to its original position behind the thigh (see Figure 37). In this way, the arm describes about three-quarters of a circle and no effort should be made to increase this or the shoulder will rise and even lock. This exercise should be repeated several times with each arm and should be done without haste and in rhythm with the horse's pace. More experienced riders can perform it with both arms at once and, later still, while the horse is cantering. Particular care should be taken that when using both arms the rider does not let the upper body swing back behind the vertical.

Figure 37 Swinging arm exercise to dispel stiffness in back and shoulders

As the waist and loins of the rider have to absorb most of the movement in the horse's back, it is most important that these muscles are truly supple. An excellent exercise for this is to place one hand in front of the saddle and the other at the back and, without allowing the hips to move, gently to reverse the position by allowing the arms to swing from back to front (see Figure 38). Done well, this is a very graceful exercise which harmonises with the canter rhythm. Care should be taken that the rider does not round his shoulder or twist in the saddle. However, no work at the canter should be attempted until the rider is really secure otherwise he will begin to introduce grip again, instead of sitting quietly down, as the horse's leading hind leg touches the ground, and allowing himself to be carried upwards and forwards by the horse's movement. Any rocking of the upper body should be stopped as it does not help either the horse or the rider.

Figure 38   Making the waist and loins supple

All arm-swinging exercises should be performed on both reins as it is important for the instructor to check that the outer leg position has not been affected. No exercise should be repeated more than five or six times and should always be followed by a few circles in the basic riding position or by a rest period. Before starting any exercise it is wise to go once through the procedure of 'correcting the position' as described on page 75.

Influencing the Horse

Once a rider is completely in control of himself while being lunged and can ride with ease at all three paces, he will find it interesting to discover how much his hard-won position can influence his horse's way of going, even without the use of the reins.

Firstly he will find that, because his seat is now deep and his legs hang down close to the horse's side, the top of his inner calf is now resting on the widest part of the horse's rib cage and it needs only a very slight movement to emphasise this pressure as a leg aid. Thus, while still on the circle, he will begin to appreciate the effect of the leg aids which, used together at the girth, can help to produce impulsion or, by placing the outside leg slightly behind the girth, can control the quarters and help to keep the horse 'straight'.

If the instructor now reverses his whip the rider will find that, provided he closes his legs and sits softly down into the saddle at each stride, he can not only send the horse forward but that the deeper he sits, as the horse's legs hit the ground, the greater will be the rebound

and, therefore, the height and suspension in the horse's stride. Advanced riders can make use of this either by accepting it as collection or by releasing it in the form of extension. Thus transitions between working, medium or collected paces can be practised with only passive help from the instructor.

However, such proficiency is rarely reached without years of tuition and experience. But even the average rider will discover that work on the lunge makes it possible for him to use his aids effectively and that, because he is balanced and relaxed, all horses will work more freely for him and with far less effort on his part.

It is not the aim of this book to discuss the training of horses under saddle, only to suggest that, since mount and man should work as one, basic training on the lunge is essential for both of them. As with the training of horses, work on the lunge should never become an end in itself, only a preliminary step towards true horsemanship. This applies whether the rider's ambitions lie in the realms of dressage, eventing or show-jumping.

As the 'bar' is to the ballet dancer so the lunge should be to the rider, a form of exercise and preparation for greater things. Only by constant practice and dedication can any rider hope to become a true horseman who can create strength without force and lightness without loss of control. Only with such a background can horse and rider merge into one, bringing delight to themselves and to all who watch them.

INDEX

David & Charles have a book on it

THE GOLDEN GUINEA BOOK OF HEAVY HORSES:
Past & Present
Edward Hart

We are now witnessing the resurgence of the heavy horse. On farms and in cities, by canals and on country roads, at ploughing matches and agricultural shows, the Shires, Clydesdales, Suffolks and Percherons are more and more in evidence. Here is a comprehensive account of the part played by these horses in our history, their changing role and modern occupations, along with information on vehicles, yoking and decorations, a glossary and an appendix on where to see the breeds on show.
240 × 208mm   Illustrated

THE HORSE'S HEALTH FROM A–Z:
An Equine Veterinary Dictionary
Peter D. Rossdale FRCVS and Susan M. Wreford

With veterinary language, especially concerning the horse, becoming increasingly technical, this dictionary is an invaluable reference work for all involved with the care and welfare of horses. Containing all the terms relating to the veterinary aspects of the animal, it is indispensible not only to owners, but to students, trainers and stud grooms.
234 × 156mm   Illustrated

DRESSAGE:
Begin the Right Way
Lockie Richards

How to succeed in this classical method of horse training for the average horse and rider. Techniques from basics through to more advanced movements, are described in clear and simple language, admirably illustrated by photographs of top riders in the United Kingdom, United States and Europe, and easily-followed figures.
216 × 138mm   Illustrated

THE RIDING INSTRUCTOR'S HANDBOOK
Monty Mortimer

It is estimated that over 2 million people ride at least once a week in the United Kingdom; consequently there is a greater demand than ever for qualified riding instructors. Few books on the market actually help to explain the techniques of teaching riding and *The Riding Instructor's Handbook* aims to do just that. No attempt is made to teach riding; the aim of the book is to provide the student instructor with a standard work for study, and the practising instructor with a practical reference book to aid the preparation of his lessons, right up to the level of Fellowship of the British Horse Society.
216 × 138mm   Illustrated

KEEPING YOUR HORSE HEALTHY:
The Prevention and Cure of Illnesses
Fritz Sevelius, Harry Petterson and Lennart Olsson

For all horse-owners: a comprehensive guide to the care of horses in sickness and health, with methods of treatment described step-by-step.
255 × 185mm   Illustrated

A GUIDE TO RIDING, SHOWING & ENJOYING OTHER PEOPLE'S HORSES
Barbara Burn

Most books on riding ignore the special requirements of riders who don't possess their own horse but have to rely on borrowed or hired mounts. Now, Barbara Burn tells 'horseless' riders of all ages how to assess a stable and its mounts; how to select an instructor; how to get the best out of a hired horse; what the responsibilities are of riding someone else's horse. Drawing upon the advice of expert riders and her own twenty-five years of experience of riding other people's horses, Barbara Burn proves that you don't have to own a horse to get the most out of riding.
234 × 156mm   Illustrated

HORSE BREEDING
Peter Rossdale

A leading vet in Newmarket, the cradle of thoroughbreds, Peter Rossdale is dealing constantly with men and women who are concerned with horses and the problems of breeding, although for the most part, they have little or no specialist knowledge. He has written his book for such people. It explains in simple language the biological functions on which reproduction is based for it is important, he believes, for those at all levels of responsibility in stables and stud farms to have some understanding of what goes on the better to cope with various problems they encounter.
234 × 156mm   Illustrated

BREEDING AND TRAINING A HORSE OR PONY
Anne Sutcliffe

A thoroughly practical book for anyone considering breeding from a favourite mare. It covers the five or six years from choosing a stallion to training the foal as a reliable, confident riding horse and reading for further, more specialised, training. Wise and experienced advice is given on all the different stages, including answers to such basic questions as how to decide if the mare is suitable to breed from, how to tell that the mare is ready to foal, how to load mare and foal into a horse box, how to teach the foal to tie up, and how to take him out into traffic.
216 × 138mm   Illustrated

THE HEAVY HORSE MANUAL
Nick Rayner & Keith Chivers

Having 'a good horse in the stable' is once again becoming as desirable as it is practical, but there is very little published on the subject in book form. Indeed, this may well be the first book that covers it fully. Both experts, the authors lay out the pros and cons of ownership and discuss the choice of breed, general care, breaking, training, harness and breeding – the whole gamut. This is a thoroughly down-to-earth manual that will help you to make up your own mind, be it on ownership or coping with all contingencies that arise from it.
234 × 156mm   Illustrated

FOX HUNTING
The Duke of Beaufort

The Master of England's great hunt that has borne his name for generations has given us a unique insight into the sport in all of its aspects. He has had personal experience of all the duties involved in hunt management and his accounts will enable all those taking part to have a greater understanding of their sport – and therefore deeper appreciation of it. Some seventy black and white photographs with additional colour pictures complete a classic book that will surely qualify as the standard work for decades to come.
245 × 169mm   Illustrated

RIDING AND STABLE SAFETY
Ann Brock

At last a single volume covering all aspects of safety in connection with horses and ponies. Do *you* know how to tie up your pony so that he cannot hurt himself; how to guard against accidents in the stable yard; how to behave on the public road? From safe gear for your first lesson to riding for handicapped children, it is all here: stable construction, care of tack, care of the horse in the stable and at grass, first aid, hunting, jumping and much, much more. Ann Brock writes from wide experience, and her book will be invaluable in view of the recent unprecedented spread of riding stables and of private horse ownership.
216 × 138mm   Illustrated